Chinese Snuff Bottles

A Guide to Addictive Miniatures

Trevor Cornforth

and Dr. Nathan Cheung

Schiffer Publishing Ltd®

4880 Lower Valley Road, Atglen, PA 19310 USA

Photography by Trevor Cornforth

Library of Congress Cataloging-in-Publication Data

Cornforth, Trevor W.
Chinese snuff bottles: a guide to addictive miniatures/ Trevor Cornforth and Nathan Cheung.
p. cm.
ISBN 0-7643-1591-9
1. Snuff boxes and bottles—China—Catalogs. 2. Snuff boxes and bottles—Collectors and collecting—Catalogs. I. Cheung, Nathan. II. Title.
NK9507 .C678 2002
745.593'4'0951075—dc21
2002004045

Designed by "Sue"
Type set in Zapf Humanist 601 demi BT/Korinna BT

ISBN: 0-7643-1591-9
Printed in China
1 2 3 4

Published by Schiffer Publishing Ltd.
4880 Lower Valley Road
Atglen, PA 19310
Phone: (610) 593-1777; Fax: (610) 593-2002
E-mail: Schifferbk@aol.com
Please visit our web site catalog at
www.schifferbooks.com
We are always looking for people to write books on new and related subjects. If you have an idea for a book, please contact us at the above address.

This book may be purchased from the publisher.
Include $3.95 for shipping.
Please try your bookstore first.
You may write for a free catalog.

In Europe, Schiffer books are distributed by
Bushwood Books
6 Marksbury Ave. Kew Gardens
Surrey TW9 4JF England
Phone: 44 (0)20 8392-8585; Fax: 44 (0)20 8392-9876
E-mail: Bushwd@aol.com
Free postage in the UK. Europe: air mail at cost.
Please try your bookstore first.

Acknowledgements

The writing of this book would not have been possible without the help of several individuals. We would like to thank Jo and Brian Penny, Zvi and Angela Klemer, Yan Dongmei (China Guardian Auctions Company Ltd., Beijing), Chen Xia, Matthew and Caroline Skippen, for loaning us their beautiful collections. We are also extremely grateful to Aixinjueluo (Aisingioro) Yu Lan, Li Zengming, Jin Yu and Yan Guiping in Beijing, for permission to include some of their snuff bottles in this book. We also thank Ma Jun for his photography of the snuff bottles from these Chinese collectors based in Beijing.

We have named the owner for each illustrated bottle where appropriate. However, should there be one or two bottles without the name of their owners, we sincerely apologize to the respective collector.

Before even writing the book, we must say thank you to Judy Smith for getting the ball rolling, Bob Marrion for his delightful illustration, Nik Ragg for his photographic advice, and Zhu Cui Ying (Adams) for her invaluable translation.

Finally, a huge thank you to Tintin Zheng for his ongoing and invaluable help in China.

Foreword

I was introduced to snuff bottles some years ago while on a visit to China with the authors of this book. I was immediately attracted to these lovely miniatures and have been intrigued by them ever since. The amazing variety available is almost beyond description.

I now have quite a collection, indeed some of them are featured in this book, but I am still forever on the lookout for the next irresistible find.

I have learnt quite a lot on the subject as I have gone along but up to now it has been difficult to find a comprehensive guide which was not too bogged down in detail. I believe that this book is about to put that right.

This beautifully illustrated and informative book will tell you, as it has me, all you need to know about the fascinating subject of snuff bottles. By consulting it you will be able to find out the history and price range of a bottle and I believe that after reading it you will look at your treasures through completely different eyes.

I am quite sure that the new knowledge I have acquired is going to double the pleasure I shall have from my collection now and in the future.

Jo Penny

Contents

Preface

Buying Snuff Bottles

One of the principle objects of this book is to help the buyer through the hugely complex price structure of the snuff bottle market, so it is essential that we explain how our own prices have been formulated. There are many price guides among modern collectors publications and there is an unfortunate tendency among many readers to give these guides biblical status. Neither this nor any other guide should ever be regarded as anything other than a guide and to refer to a "book price" is an unfortunate sign of people's dependency upon them, both as sellers and buyers. With snuff bottles, probably more than most other collectibles, variations in age, provenance and simple quality will be enormous, as will the variations in price. It might be assumed that the disparity between some of the auction prices quoted here and the general selling prices can be explained by their age and authenticity. Though this should be, and in some instances is, the case many bottles have gained inappropriate credibility through appearing in well-known auctions. The purchasers may therefore have been duped into paying a high premium for a newly acquired provenance (that is, the auction room) where no previous provenance or indeed significant history would have enhanced their price. The expression *caveat emptor* or buyer beware is much more applicable when dealing with large sums of money than small. It is easy to justify paying a few tens or even hundreds of pounds for an item simply because you like it but when the sum involved runs into thousands it is a different matter.

There are two basic groups of bottles and prices featured within this text. The first is a selection of bottles which have appeared in internationally important auctions within China. As such these bottles have received worldwide publicity and the expert assessment of Chinese specialists. While buyers from around the world are welcome to attend, and frequently do, it is particularly interesting to note that the majority of buyers are Chinese nationals. This, in itself, demonstrates that the modern market is not dictated by the budget of the Western collector and enthusiast. Prices appearing with, for example, (A) £1,000 beneath them have been sold within the last five years in auction for that price. Other bottles appearing with (A) £1,000-£1,500 have either failed to achieve the auctioneer's estimated price, for whatever reason, or have not yet been offered for sale at the time of writing but have this guide price in the auctioneer's catalogue. Comparisons of bottles sold with their estimated prices suggest that the majority were realistically estimated. Where that is not the case we have indicated both achieved and estimated prices.

It has also been interesting to find that, particularly since our entry into the twenty-first century, many of the leading auction houses in the west have begun to offer, what are described as, twentieth century bottles in their sales. With nothing more to go on, by way of age or provenance, it becomes the buyer who must decide whether the item offered is of suitable quality or has any history. With such a loose description the bottles concerned may be completely new, which is not in itself a problem, but seems to be contrary to the usual policy of such famous "rooms." Once sold, of course, whatever the age of the bottle, it will then have a provenance because it was important enough to have been included in such a sale.

The second group of bottles is not known to us to have appeared in auction but belong to our own or other private collections or are currently being offered for sale within the collectors' market. Prices within this market vary hugely, often according to the credibility of the seller and their location. Such variations are not unique to snuff bottles and should encourage the collector to step outside their familiar safe territory and explore the availability of pieces in other parts of a country or its markets. Prices shown beneath these photographs will simply indicate a suitable band such as £1,000-£1,500 which in our experience is appropriate. Many dealers may consider these prices to be too low and will seek to justify theirs being higher by suggesting significant provenance or the importance to their own reputation. The simple fact is that neither we, nor anyone else, fix prices and the qualities which determine price are so variable that each must be assessed individually.

In China a bottle depicting a five-toed dragon will be rated more highly than another which has only four toes. There may be little or no difference in the quality of the product but the former will be seen as more desirable. In the West such information will have little credibility with collectors being far more interested in provenance and hopefully quality.

It must be remembered that very few snuff bottles are mass-produced. The vast majority, even today, are produced in small workshops and crafts studios by highly skilled artisans with the result that each bottle is unique. While many subjects may be repeated and some artisans will specialize in dragons, calligraphy or some other detail, each bottle requires many hours of work and becomes a unique work of art.

The word provenance has already been mentioned several times and forms an additional influence upon the price structure of any piece be it a snuff bottle or a string of pearls. An item of jewelry once worn by *Marilyn Monroe* may fetch a thousand times more than might be expected for a similar item owned and worn by *Jane Doe*. Similarly a snuff bottle known to have been in the possession of an Emperor or high official of the Qing Court will reach astronomic heights if offered for open sale. Even a bottle which can be shown to have been in a well documented private collection for many years will have achieved significant credibility. The majority of important bottles, however, have remained in museum displays since the end of the Qing dynasty and so do not come on the market. Having said that it is perfectly feasible that a simple bottle once handled by a Qing nobleman slipped the net in the chaos and confusion of the early twentieth century and now languishes unrecognized in a shop or less well known collection.

Advice for Buyers and Collectors

Given the variety of design and materials of snuff bottles available, both contemporary and antique, it may seem daunting for the beginner to know where to begin acquiring some of these little gems. As we have mentioned earlier, if a bottle takes your fancy, you can afford it and are willing to part with the money, then indulge yourself and buy it. In this way you buy the bottles you want in your collection and get the maximum enjoyment out of them. It seems a shame to be in possession of a particular type of bottle just to "complete" the collection even though you do not particularly like it or it is of poor quality. Cheaper snuff bottles should not always be dismissed, simply because you perceive their price as too low. The price may not reflect the quality of the bottle and you could have a bargain in your hands. Even dealers who know their subject may not be asking full market price because they don't have direct access to those who will pay it. The prices given as indications in this book do not necessarily reflect those we might ask ourselves but are a fair indication of what you can expect to pay in the general market.

In any good collection one should always be prepared to get rid of the pieces which no longer hold your interest or are surpassed in beauty by others. Not only is this practical, as some of your bottles can be re-sold to fund others, but you may otherwise fool yourself in to thinking that your collection is complete, in number terms if not variety and quality.

A good starting point to buy snuff bottles would be at local auctions or if your bank account allows it, at larger auction houses. For the majority of us, an excellent place to scout for snuff bottles would be at antique fairs, shops and centers. A good dealer will be prepared to spend time explaining the subject and pointing out the qualities of the items for sale. However, beware of being persuaded to buy a particular piece because it may be one he wants rid of. Better to listen to the details offered and then decide on the basis of merit and, ultimately, whether you like it.

When buying snuff bottles nothing beats actually handling, seeing and sensing the qualities of each piece. No illustration can ever replace this contact. We believe that this contact is more than just physical. A connection must be made between you and the bottle, and it is you who decides whether it becomes a "must have" or not.

Mistakes in purchases happen, everyone makes them whether beginners or experienced collectors, because that is the very nature of collecting. We all learn by our mistakes and this ultimately creates a better collection. Simply try to avoid such mistakes being too expensive by being very cautious indeed when it comes to the higher priced items.

If anything is to be taken away from this chapter for buyers and collectors, especially for those new to snuff bottles, it should be to look for quality in any piece. Perhaps the word "quality" should be underlined, as this ought to be the determining factor in whether you part with your money. It is, for instance, arguably better to buy a good contemporary bottle than a poor earlier one. There are three basic factors in evaluating any given snuff bottle, they being the physical properties, aesthetic properties and extrinsic properties of the piece in question.

The physical properties to look out for include identification and quality of the material, and the condition of the bottle. The bottle may be damaged or have flaws in the material. Damage may not be so much a reflection of its age, as the possible deliberate distressing to give the impression of age. It is also important to look out for any repair which may have been carried out on a bottle as this can obviously affect the price. In addition, some stone snuff bottles may have been dyed to look like jade and some jade ones dyed to improve their color. The latter may be considered less serious since, historically, staining and coloring have been traditional methods of enhancing apparent quality.

The aesthetic properties include factors such as craftsmanship, color and type of bottle, style, period characteristics, and in some instances the school or groups of artist where certain bottles were produced. It is the carving or more precisely the "working" in a snuff bottle which ranks highest in this list. However, ornamentation may not necessarily give a bottle merit, importance or beauty, as observed in some jade snuff bottles, where the working with respect to carving is minimal. It is apt here to suggest that there is no need to "gild the lily." In these instances the artist has exercised restraint and thus allowed the natural qualities of the stone, its form and natural markings, to speak for themselves.

The extrinsic properties include intangible factors such as a verifiable history or provenance, market demand, local taste and the rarity of a given bottle. It is often difficult, almost impossible, to obtain reliable provenance of a piece. Many dealers may use such emotive words as "Ming" or phrases such as "Reign of Qianlong," but do not be easily swayed. As mentioned before, it is almost impossible to date by eye the age of any snuff bottle. Does the seller know where the subject bottle has been for the last fifty years or so? If no, then can a three, four or even five figure price be justified? Factors such as market demand, local taste and the rarity of the bottle may govern your choice in whether to buy the bottle or not, especially if you are considering your collection to be a financial investment.

All collectors place differing levels of importance on each of these properties but they do at least provide a framework in the decision making process. We strongly recommend that you judge any collectible, be it snuff bottles or other items you collect, firstly on their tangible qualities (physical and aesthetic), and then on their intangible or extrinsic properties before any decision is made. The summation of these issues comes down to questions of quality, possibly age and your enthusiasm to achieve a stunning collection. Happy collecting!

Introduction

The vast majority of snuff bottles were, and still are, made in China. While snuff itself was not a Chinese product, the small bottles and lids with elongated miniature spoons used to ladle it out certainly were.

They can be variously described as fascinating, attractive, exotic, in some cases even awesome but all are a delight to look at, hold and collect. The casual observer of existing books on the subject and some of the collections now made famous might be forgiven for steering clear of snuff bottles as a potential collector's item. Many early and special examples will certainly cost an arm and a leg to acquire, and even one may be beyond the budget of the modest collector let alone a whole collection, but less important and later examples can be obtained for just a little toe.

In the text which follows we have catalogued numerous examples of snuff bottles not previously documented and which mostly fall below the very high price bracket. Some, particularly those which have appeared in international auctions, will run into the low thousands of pounds but others begin at little more than a child's pocket money.

Although perhaps beyond the general study of most children, the collecting of these lovely objects undoubtedly opens the way to an understanding of an ancient culture which in recent years has been brought rapidly into line with the rest of the world.

The history of the snuff bottle is relatively recent in Chinese terms and so does not require a deep knowledge of the country's long and complicated past. Instead one can begin with the arrival of the Qing Dynasty (pronounced Ching) in 1644, upon the demise of the Ming, and it has therefore only been necessary for us to chart the Emperors of that last dynasty until its own demise in 1912.

Almost in contradiction of the last paragraph snuff bottles, as an art form, give an insight into China's culture prior to 1644 and also the years after the revolution which brought about the end of Imperial rule. Much of the decoration used dates back into its long history and then rushes forward to the present day as some artists have been influenced by the work of their foreign contemporaries.

Despite assertions to the contrary, by some dealers, a snuff bottle cannot therefore be more than four hundred years old and this will become more apparent in the chapter dealing with the history and development of snuff taking itself.

Throughout the text there will be references to Chinese names and expressions for which we have used the modern Pinyin spellings. These have been developed, particularly in relation to the official Mandarin dialect, as a phonetic interpretation of the sounds used in the Chinese language. It is unlikely that most collectors will wish to learn Chinese simply in order to enhance their knowledge of the culture but this should add to their enjoyment by at least knowing an approximation of names and words associated with the bottles. In referring to other books mentioned in the Bibliography the reader may well be confused by the variations used in older texts. For example, the first Qing Emperor is here referred to as Shunzhi but in earlier texts will appear as Hsun-chih. Some books, in particular those printed in China, may refer to an Emperor by his pre-Imperial name. This can be even more confusing, hence our own use of the more familiar modern spellings. A full list of Emperors from 1644 to 1912 will be found in the History chapter.

We shall also differ considerably from most other books on the subject in giving significant credibility to bottles produced after the end of the Qing and right up to the present day. Many of the "old school" of collectors claim only to be interested in bottles "made for use" and refer to the later examples as "just made for tourists". We prefer to think of snuff bottles as an ongoing art form which has evolved into the twentieth and now the twenty-first centuries. They may well include inexpensive mass produced pieces which are within the budget and the carrying capacity of the tourist but it also includes exquisite works by craftsmen and women whose families have produced similar items for many generations. It is these later bottles and some of the less exotic earlier ones which are within the budget of the modest modern collector. It is also highly questionable whether all of the early examples would have been intended for use, since they quickly caught the imaginations of collectors from the Emperor downwards, and became admired collectors pieces rather than every day objects.

In researching for this book we have encountered a whole new breed of serious buyers who are prepared to spend, sometimes large, sums of money to acquire unique pieces which they know were made "yesterday". A large number of those collectors are in the Far East but some we have encountered have been purchasing for ongoing museum and gallery collections in both East and West. It is therefore safe to assume that we are by no means the only people giving credibility to the modern bottle.

We are obviously indebted to the various writers whose books appear in the Bibliography and certainly would recommend that anyone wishing to broaden their knowledge should refer to them. Some detail the acquisitions of a particular collection and others place their emphasis on the history of these strange miniature containers. Our aim is to give the reader a broad general understanding of the history of snuff taking, the development of the snuff bottle and the many forms it can take. To avoid lengthy explanations and an over indulgent text much of the information to be gathered is included with the photographs. This will also avoid the reader having to flick from page to page when reading the text in order to see the pieces referred to. We hope this will make our book reader-friendly.

Inevitably some of the "old school" will dismiss the book as irrelevant to them but at the same time we do feel we offer new insights which even they may wish to take on board. We should, however, certainly appeal to the more recent or new collector who perhaps will follow the same lines as we have and appreciate the guidance.

Chapter by chapter we have attempted to deal with as many as possible of the questions regularly asked by buyers and frequently remaining unanswered by less knowledgeable sellers. We have combined the text, much of the time, with the photographs in order to make for ready reference for both parties. Even experts find some materials difficult to properly identify, especially within the stone category where geological and generic terms overlap, so it is with some trepidation that we have defined all bottles as precisely as possible. It is interesting to note that most auction catalogues, however, are as vague as possible and group all jade-like stones together as jade and refer to other materials with the barest detail.

In this respect, illustrated bottles which have appeared, or are due to appear, in auction are described exactly as they are in the relevant catalogues.

Most snuff bottles are around the same size, being between 2.5" (6.5cms) and 3.5" (9cms) in height and consequently have not been detailed more accurately in the text, but where they fall outside those measurements the size is specified.

Chapter One: A History of Snuff Taking

Sixteenth Century

"Native American Invention"

The tobacco from which snuff is made is not indigenous to China any more than it was in Europe, and it is the arrival of it where our story really begins. Tobacco arrived in Europe in the sixteenth century after the discovery of the Americas and quickly became a fashion accessory for the rich and famous. It was an expensive product which had great mystery and risk attached to its acquisition because of the lengthy journeys across the Atlantic in fragile ships.

Learning from the Native Americans, who had used it for centuries, the merchants marketed it in three main forms. The most common today is smoking tobacco as cigarettes and for pipes but at the time of its arrival it was better known for chewing and sniffing. It is the sniffing of powdered tobacco which concerns us here and this quickly became a habit of the gentility, including the ladies. Snuff, as it was called, was reputed to have medicinal properties which enhanced its reputation and encouraged its use among women as well as men.

"European Addiction"

From the Royal houses of Europe down to the merchants of the day snuff taking, or snuffing, became a popular pastime and, of course, an addiction. To enhance this pleasure a wide selection of containers were made in the form of small boxes, usually with hinged lids, in a wide variety of materials. From the jeweled gold versions of the aristocracy to the decorated silver of the merchants' wives and the simpler wood of many of the men, these became treasured possessions passed from friend to colleague and back in the ritual of "partaking of a little snuff." A minor industry grew around the habit as snuffboxes became ready gifts and fashion items. Hence the modern collector has a vast array to choose from though the majority of the best examples remain behind glass in the stately homes and museums of the world.

Seventeenth Century

"Chinese Imperial Pleasure"

It should be no surprise that eventually snuff reached China, probably around the 1630's, just before the end of the Ming Dynasty. A decree in 1639 had attempted to ban the use of smoking tobacco but failed and snuff offered an alternative which was less easily detected. Snuff taking in China probably began in the north with the Manchus who overthrew the Ming emperors and installed themselves as the Qing Dynasty in 1644.

Emperors of the Qing dynasty (1644-1912):

Emperor	**Reign**
Shunzhi (*Hsun-chih*)	1644-1661
Kangxi (*K'ang-hsi*)	1662-1722
Yongzheng (*Yung-cheng*)	1723-1735
Qianlong (*Ch'ien-lung*)	1736-1795
Jiaqing (*Chia-ch'ing*)	1796-1820
Daoguang (*Tao-kuang*)	1821-1850
Xianfeng (*Hsien-feng*)	1851-1861
Tongzhi (*T'ung-chih*)	1862-1874
Guangxu (*Kuang-hsu*)	1875-1908
Xuantong (*Hsuan-t'ung*)	1909-1911

Of course it would not have gone directly to the Imperial Court and may well have languished around the docks and ports for some time. British, Spanish and Portuguese merchant ships were regular visitors to Chinese shores by this time seeking out the valuable porcelain and tea so fashionable at home. The habits of the foreigners would have been observed and with the reputed medicinal properties may well have attracted the early attention of the local doctors to whom powdered plants and natural remedies were nothing new. It would have been a natural step for them to try to add this new wonder to their list of potions and the visiting merchants would have been equally quick to recognize an opportunity.

It is also possible that the doctors were beaten to this new product by local merchants anxious to promote their business with something so obviously popular among the foreigners. Either way it eventually reached the nose of the Emperor and found approval. Once that had happened, of course, the result was the same as in Europe and snuff became a fashion item with those who could afford it anxious to show that they shared the Emperor's taste.

Eighteenth Century

"Snuff's Peak of Popularity"

The first known record of snuff bottles appears in a book entitled *Xiang Zu Bi Ji* (Notes to a Fragrant Ancestor) written by *Wang Shizhen*, a high ranking minister in the court of Emperor Kangxi. It was written in the forty-second and forty-third years (1703-1704) of the Emperor's long reign, after *Wang's* retirement and speaks of snuff having been recently "produced" in the Capital and that it was supposed to improve sight and "exorcise" epidemic diseases. He also refers to the storage and carrying of the snuff in colored glass bottles and to it being inhaled from a small ivory spoon. Other evidence and the setting up of a glass workshop in the Forbidden City in 1696 suggest that both snuff and the bottles were well established at the time of *Wang's* writing.

Why then did the snuffers of China not choose to use the same small boxes as their European counterparts since that must have been the way in which it was first introduced? The answer gives us a clue that it was probably the doctors who first recognized its potential and brought it to the Imperial nostril.

In the mid-seventeenth century and even to the present day herbal medicines were usually dispensed in small ceramic bottles with small necks and tight fitting lids or stoppers. When the contents were to be mixed with water and ingested it was fine to tip the bottle to empty the contents into a cup, be they liquid or powder. As the contents were to be sniffed, however, this was less satisfactory so a long spoon was developed to allow a measured dose to be removed.

The European habit was, and still is, to take a pinch between thumb and forefinger and then either inhale directly or place the powder on the back of the hand and inhale from there. In either case this was neither a measured dose nor a particularly attractive method of taking it, resulting in excess brown powder staining the nostrils and any moustache. This would certainly not have been acceptable to the rather precise Chinese mind especially as the fashion at the time was for the Emperor and his subjects to have long moustaches. From the medicine bottle then came the habit of transferring a much smaller dose of snuff onto the thumbnail, *via* the small spoon, which could then be cleanly sniffed with little or no residue.

"Snuff Bottles"

The snuff bottle was born as result of a marriage between a western product and the eastern culture and, in much the same way as in Europe, a whole new craft industry was born with it. Known as the "snuff bottle period" it therefore marked the rise and fall of the Qing Court with each successive emperor adding his own enthusiasm to a growing collection. Having begun in the reign of the Emperor Shunzhi snuffing and the collecting of the bottles had their peak during the following three reigns, Kangxi (1662-1722), Yongzhen (1723-1735) and Qianlong (1736-1795).Whether these three were great snuffers we do not know but the extensive records of the Forbidden City for the periods show that large amounts of snuff were ordered and also received as gifts but similarly large amounts were also given as gifts to foreign dignitaries and those who met with

Imperial favor. What is much more clearly stated is that the Emperors took great personal interest in the design and production of snuff bottles, especially those destined for their own collections.

Though the reasons are unknown, Kangxi tried several times during his reign to stamp out the smoking of tobacco by issuing edicts to that effect but never included snuff. This probably reflected a personal prejudice against people smoking in the Imperial presence and the likelihood that his family and courtiers would take up the habit.

To satisfy his own requirements Kangxi created workshops within the Forbidden City under the highly regarded Manufacture Department or *Zaobanshu*. He also imported craftsmen from across China and beyond. In this way they could observe and direct the work in a way unprecedented for other products. Prior to and even after the setting up of the Imperial Workshops, bottles had been ordered from many parts of the country where specialists had established themselves for centuries. The famous porcelain factories of Jingdezhen and Canton had already begun to recognize a new market as had the ivory carvers of Suzhou and the lapidaries of some of the western cities. Some of their best workers were either forced or encouraged to move to the capital to work directly for the Emperor but their output was negligible compared to the soaring demand.

Records indicate that the Forbidden City alone accounted for thousands of bottles per year, some made to order, others made as gifts and tributes on special occasions such as the annual festivals or Imperial birthdays. Many of these would have been extremely exotic but others remained simple relying on their color or tactile qualities to please. So anxious were the Emperors to have the widest choice and the best quality that they imported craftsmen from Japan, France and Germany to augment and teach their own workers.

Drawing by Bob Marrion

Under *Zaobanchu* extensive records were kept from the reign of Yongzhen onwards to almost the end of the dynasty. The ultimate destination of many of the products, including snuff bottles is also recorded indicating that a high percentage were presented by the Emperors to foreign dignitaries, officials, ministers and other important people including regularly the Dalai Lama in Tibet.

Imperial Bottles

Three specific categories of bottle emerged. Firstly those ordered and supervised by the Emperor, for which drawings would be made and submitted to him along with wooden models and prototypes. These would presumably have been for his personal use or to mark a special gift. Such bottles are rarely seen and bear a reign mark and other characters indicating that they were specifically ordered.

Presentation Bottles

The second category was of bottles designed for presentation on one of the three annual festivals *Duanwu* (Dragon Boat), *Wanshou* (Longevity) and *Nianjie* (New Year). This particular group became dominant and received great attention. An order given in the second year of Emperor Yongzhen's reign by Prince *Yi Yuangxiang* (twenty-second son of Kangxi) specified that all workshops were to produce items for the three festivals. From that time onwards it became regular practice to meet those deadlines.

An old porcelain medicine bottle with a five character mark indicating the name of the dispensary. £40-50. $55-70

Yearly Work

The third category was known as "yearly work" and consisted of the remaining bottles produced without specific purpose but for the Emperor's general use. This must have offered great creative opportunity to the workshop artisans, who would be under less constraints but, who may well have produced pieces which later caught the Emperor's keen eye and thus brought recognition for themselves. Few, however, of the individuals who worked there ever achieved the status of being able to sign their work, most of it, if marked at all, simply showing the Emperor's title and year of his reign. The few exceptions are referred to when the different types of bottle are discussed.

As the demand grew other workshops outside the Forbidden City sprang up with the majority producing bottles for the wider market but some were comparable with their more auspicious counterparts. In addition, as the craftsmen of the court returned home or retired they inevitably passed on their skills and ideas as well as the interest in taking snuff. Hence a national industry grew.

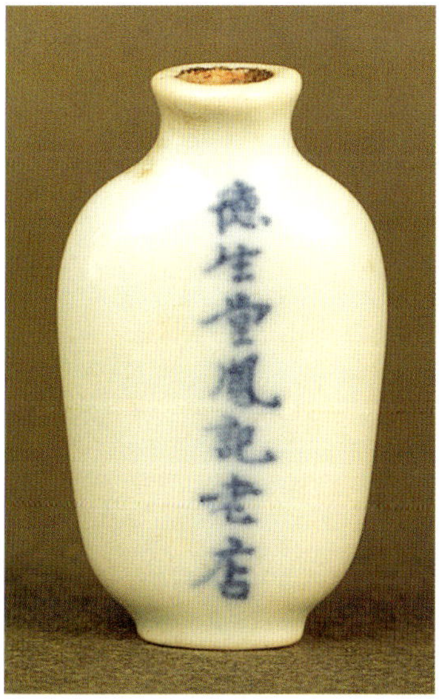

Left:
A simple medicine bottle with characters reading "*de sheng tang fen ji lao dian*". "*De sheng tang*" is a place name, possibly a group of medicine shops, or the name of a group similar to a modern franchise. "*Fen ji*" (phoenix) is a specific family or shop name and "*lao dian*" simply means "old shop". £40-50. $55-70

Right and above right:
The four characters on this medicine bottle read "*qong man ru sheng*", translating as "very good like God". This is likely to have been the name adopted by a temple dispensary and intended to indicate the quality of their medicines. £40-50. $55-70

Cabinet Bottles

In addition to the small snuff bottles designed to be carried with the taker, a number exist which are referred to as "cabinet bottles". These much larger examples were probably passed around dinner tables and at meetings as part of the social ritual and no doubt among the wealthy and elite there would have been much debate about the merits of different flavors of snuff and the relative merits of each owner's bottles. With the cabinet bottles went small dishes, sometimes referred to as snuff saucers, which were passed from person to person with each probably preferring to use his own snuff spoon. Few records exist of these delightful little bowls in either contemporary or modern writings and even fewer examples are available to buy or use for illustrative purposes.

Nineteenth Century

"Mass Appeal"

In both China and Europe interest in snuffing for the elite waned during the nineteenth century, probably because the price of tobacco fell and it became more readily available to the masses. While the habit of taking it may have diminished, in China, the interest in collecting the bottles continued in the Palace almost unabated until the end of Imperial rule in 1912. The last Emperor Xuantong was still a boy when he was deposed but remained resident in the Forbidden City until 1924.

Above and right:
This simple carved bamboo bottle probably held a commercial brand of snuff which could be decanted to a more lavish container or used directly. The characters used are archaic in style and read "*qi sang*" translating as "strange or different enjoy." a clear temptation for someone to try the product. The water lily flower floating on a pond on the reverse symbolizes a good person who may have emerged from a less good background. The implication for the buyer would be that using this product would enable them to better themselves. Nineteenth century. £40-50. $55-70

Twentieth Century

"Renewed Use"

Records of the latter years in the Palace are more sketchy and many were destroyed to cover up theft by the eunuchs and Palace officials. Many bottles were also probably sold along with other treasures to maintain the lavish lifestyle and large numbers of dependents the Imperial Household retained, even to the last. By this stage government support had dwindled and the money had to be found somewhere else. From the vast numbers of snuff bottles which clearly had been accumulated, only about three thousand remain in what is now known as the Palace Museum in Beijing. A large percentage of the finest bottles have been amassed in the Palace Museum, Taipei, Taiwan.

A small old tin of snuff sits besides a relatively modern but pretty smoked glass bottle, probably for medicine, which has been hand-enameled.

Since the taking of snuff and the subsequent production and collection of snuff bottles during the Qing dynasty developed into a popular gentlemanly pursuit, it may have been viewed by many during China's years of political upheaval following the last Emperor, as a relic of capitalist *bourgeois* decadence and extravagance, as only the wealthy and powerful could indulge in such treasures. It is strange and interesting then to observe a resurgence of snuff bottle production during China's Cultural Revolution of the late 1960s and early 1970s. Chairman *Mao Zedong* himself had supervised the setting up of new workshops to restore the arts associated with snuff bottles several years earlier. The production of snuff bottles may have been allowed during this time for a number of reasons. It is conceivable that snuff bottles were used as vehicles for Communist propaganda and ideology. In essence, snuff bottles symbolized and encapsulated the ethic of hard work and honest toil to produce a thing of beauty. This may have been a simple but clear

Left and below:
A carved wooden snuff bowl in the form of a lotus leaf with curled edges attached to a lotus pod and with an insect and a fish on its surface. £30-40. $40-55

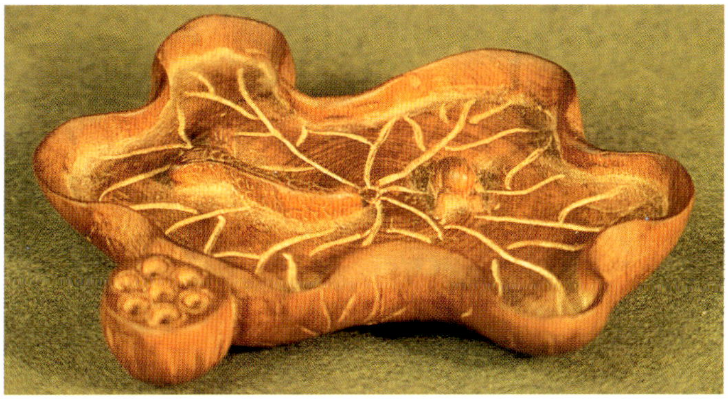

message to the common people at the time; work hard to make your country beautiful. Snuff bottles and their creation may therefore also have been a source of national pride and a reflection of the high quality of crafts skills which the country still had to offer. Their charm and attraction may also have been too much for their collectors and admirers to relinquish despite drastic changes to China's social and economic situation.

The art of production, for whatever reason, has survived and flourished with modern demand both at home and abroad. Many of the families producing excellent work today do so because of the skills passed from generation to generation even through the years of strife and hardship. While it may be appropriate to dismiss a few as tourist fodder it is an insult to the skill and artistry of the current producers to ignore them. Many artists should be ranked as highly in snuff bottle terms as their western contemporaries who weald a paint brush, sign their names and demand or command large prices in the art market.

Pages 20, 21, and 22:
A selection of hand-painted modern enamel snuff bowls with various designs. Even modern versions are hard to obtain. £25 each. $35 each.

Chapter Two: Decoration & Symbolism in Chinese Art

The snuff bottle is and always has been a "canvas" for the artist, be they painter, carver, sculptor or general craftsman. As such the enormity of Chinese art history was at their fingertips though until recently there was little opportunity for self-expression because all Chinese art forms have been dominated by symbolism, history and legend. Each of these in turn reflects the common aspirations of the people for long life, health, wealth and happiness and their wishes to that effect for their peers and betters.

Throughout all traditional Chinese art, therefore, runs a theme of visual images based upon those aspirations and it is sometimes difficult to establish why a particular association has been made. Many are based on "homonyms" or word puns which are common in Chinese because of its use of similar sounds with tonal variations for totally different things. In addition the combination of two sounds may produce yet another meaning. For example the word "*xiong*" for bear combined with "*ying*" for eagle produces the basic word for "hero". While the written characters bear little or no resemblance to the homonym the sounds do.

In an attempt to help the reader gain more enjoyment from this aspect of a collection we have set out a selection of the more commonly encountered examples. Regrettably but inevitably any such list will be incomplete and would require an entire study of Chinese art history to be otherwise. Safe to say though that almost no bottle has been produced with outer or inner decoration or embellishment without there being some degree of symbolism attached to it. The only likely exceptions are portrait bottles and those few with abstract designs. Even in these exceptions the uses of color or dress style can have deeper meaning than is immediately obvious. Thus the snuff bottle must be regarded as not just a decorative container but also an amulet designed to invoke for the carrier the traits or circumstances borne on it.

In addition to the list below details are given with many bottles so that the combination of the two will enable the reader to research and enjoy the decoration on pieces seen elsewhere.

It should be clear from the complexity and cross-association of the symbols that there was little chance of the commercial artist producing a work suitable for all occasions. It is far more likely that the majority of bottles were decorated to order with the particular images to be used being agreed in advance by the person commissioning the piece. Even modern bottles stick rigidly to the symbolism of the past and are not simply replicas of works seen by the creator.

The list of symbols is almost endless with almost every creature and plant, mountain, and stretch of water in China having some meaning or other. Simply adding clouds, rippled or still water, mountains or rice grains to these symbols enhance them or change them completely. Each was obviously a stimulus for both the artist and the person commissioning the work. It must have been a long labor of study for the artist to get to grips with all the symbolic tools available to him.

The Yin and Yang Symbol

The well known Yin and Yang symbol associated now with the art of *Feng Shui* represents the balance of positivity and negativity. Also seen as a symbol of the balance of male and female its main association is with the dualism of the universe itself. It is therefore a scholarly design which may be given at a time of life crisis or when the recipient is entering a period of study.

The Eighteen Lohan

Known as The Eighteen Scholars who rode to Yingjow these followers of the Buddha were mortal but are credited with supernatural powers. They are frequently depicted singly in various poses which have become associated with each individual and his particular gifts or as a total or part group. The particular symbolism associated with the use of one or more of these characters can be quite complex. Such decoration was often used in gifts for candidates sitting the Imperial Examination or as a gift after success in the same.

The Eight Immortals

Similar to the Lohan the Eight Immortals of Taoism are colorful and symbolic characters frequently used in Chinese art. They have more specifically defined roles in relation to poverty, wealth, aristocracy, common birth, age, youth, masculinity and femininity. Each is also associated with a non-human symbol such as a fan, scroll, sword, castanets, flower basket, drum, flute and lotus, or gourd and when the symbols alone are seen they are known as The Eight Hidden Immortals. Probably best known in the West is *Shou Lao* (correct name *Zhang Guo Lao* but also known in Chinese as *Lao Shou Xing*) whose extra large head and long gnarled staff is associated with old age and wisdom. He should more correctly be referred to as *Lao Shou* since the word "*lao*" means old and "*Shou*" has become his name. The fact that he is used more than any other Immortal in Chinese art is evidence of the Chinese reverence for age, wisdom and experience.

The Eight Buddhist Emblems

Similar to the Taoist emblems these may be seen instead of the human representations as the wheel or bell, conch, umbrella, canopy, lotus, vase, pair of fish, and endless knots of entrails.

The Bat

The Chinese word for bat "*fu*" is similar in sound to the word "*fu*" meaning happiness, with tonal variations, with the result that the bat is used to represent and invoke happiness. The commonly seen image of five bats flying is known as The Five Blessings, those being longevity, wealth, health, love of virtue and accomplishment. When seen in iron-red decoration the bat becomes "huge fortune" by combining the words "*hong*" (red) and "*fu*" (good luck or fortune). Its association with the Buddhist or Taoist emblems will imply that in order to gain the luck associated with the bat, the qualities associated with the emblem should be practiced. The bats with a fan, for example, entreat the recipient to do charitable works in order to gain luck. Endless variations of inclusion of a bat or bats in the design show the importance of this creature. Conversely, in Southern China where the language is Cantonese the bat is seen as a symbol of bad luck and superstition.

The Dragon

Probably best known of all Chinese symbols the dragon takes numerous forms and has different numbers of toes. The complexity of dragon symbolism requires almost a book of its own but suffice to say the dragon is normally associated with the Emperor. The larger the number of toes the higher his rank and he may be associated with the sky, the water or mountains. His symbolism, as with the role of the Emperor, links him with strength, power, protection, vigilance and goodness. In his more stylized and less obvious form he is often mistaken for a lesser creature such as a tiger or panther but can be recognized by the fact that his tail splits into three or more separate tails.

The dragon can appear in female form, but is hard to distinguish. Two dragons playing usually implies one of each sex for balance and completeness.

The Phoenix

Generally associated with the Empress the phoenix is often seen as the balance to the dragon. In fact the union of the dragon and the phoenix is seen as a perfect match which would take place in the clouds or a celestial environment. As such it is both impossible and lucky beyond imagination.

The phoenix like the dragon has both male and female forms with the result that the phoenix is often seen without the dragon where it is associated with the sun, warmth, summer and the harvest.

The One Hundred Children

Based upon two famous paintings, one by *Su Han Chung* of the Song dynasty and *Ding Yuen Pung* of the Ming dynasty, it has become a popular subject for Chinese art generally and snuff bottles in particular. As all of the children are generally seen to be boys it reflects the historic preference for boy children rather than girls and is associated with the desire for fertility. Given as a wedding gift the implications are obvious. While known as The One Hundred Children the numbers may be as small as ten, the number being symbolic rather than actual.

The Chinese Lion Dogs

Referred to as "*fo*" or "*fu*" they are generally seen in pairs, with one representing the male and the other the female. The male dog may have a ball (known as a "*chu*") in its mouth or beneath its paw. Overlaid with a Yin and Yang symbol at times this is intended to represent his life essence. The ball may also be overlaid with a symbol of several coins or cash. His partner the female dog is usually seen protecting a cub. The two are seen as emblems of bravery, energy and strength and would be given in recognition of those qualities or to invoke them in a child or sibling. A single lion dog of either sex would imply congratulations for attaining the top rank in the Imperial Examinations.

The Year Signs

With their twelve year cycle and associations with birthdays these are an obvious source of decoration for the craftsman since any piece with any of the twelve represented on it is a potential birthday gift. Each of the twelve animals has additional associations beyond that of the year sign and will frequently be combined with other symbols listed above or not yet covered.

While the monkey may be associated with guile and trickery, it is revered by Buddhists. The horse lays claim to speed, power and perseverance. When the two are linked and the monkey is seen riding the horse the association is with an immediate title of nobility. It may well be that such a bottle would have been given by the Emperor prior to his bestowing the honor of a title on an individual.

The ox is used in association with spring and agriculture as well as hard work and strength but he is also regularly depicted with a boy riding on his back. The tiger, representing a rank of nobility immediately below that of the Emperor, is a popular subject depicted on the ground beneath a flying dragon thus indicating loyalty of the subject tiger for the Emperor dragon.

The Stork, Crane and Deer

All three are symbolic of longevity with the crane as a paired bird particularly important as a long life wish for a newly married couple.

The Western idea of the stork being associated with babies has no place in Chinese symbolism despite the representation by many Western dealers to the contrary.

The Cat and The Butterfly

The cat *"mow"* means "live to eighty or ninety years" and the butterfly *"dai er"* means "live seventy or eighty years." It would seem rather strange and ill mannered to give someone the symbol of a butterfly instead of a cat but in fact the two symbols are usually combined or are in pairs thus significantly increasing the wished lifespan. Multiples of either thus wish longevity beyond that which is humanly possible.

The Elephant

Like several other symbols it is the sound association between *"xiang"* (elephant) and *"xiang"* (auspicious) which gives us the most important link to its usage but it should be no surprise that the elephant also stands for wisdom, prudence and power. An item given with an elephant as the principle decoration would indicate a very special occasion and perhaps one of mental or physical victory.

The Cockerel

As well as being a year sign, the cockerel with its cockscomb proudly raised is the sign of a dignitary and would be given as a congratulation at a time of promotion.

The Melon

Usually a Chinese bitter melon depicted with tendrils is a sign of continuing prosperity and would be a gift between business associates.

The Tortoise

It is probably not surprising that this long living creature should be associated with longevity and endurance. Both Chinese and Hindus in fact recognize it as a representation of the universe. Many memorial tablets and bronzes in Imperial locations depict the tortoise with other creatures and even humans on its back thus increasing the strength of any symbolism associated with them.

The Bear

The bravery and strength of the bear need little explanation nor does the Chinese association with those qualities. It is hardly surprising then that when shown together the bear and the eagle are associated with a hero and thus bravery and courage. The eagle trying to swoop on a bear or the bear fending him off is seen as symbolic of an intellectual competition between them as heroes. Two bears watching each other or standing their ground has a similar implication.

The Three-legged Toad or *Chan*

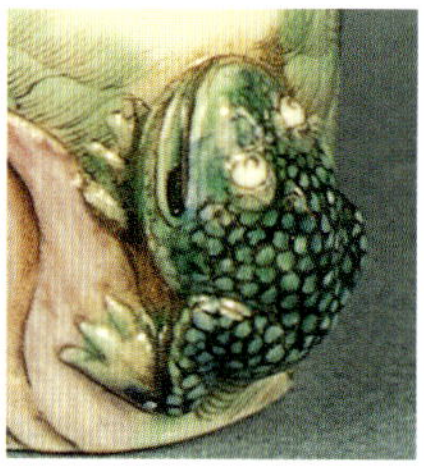

The three-legged toad known as *Chan* or *Chen* is linked with the sound of the word "*qian*" meaning money. He is also associated with the legend of *Liu Hai*, the immortal who looked after this strange creature. Said to have been a minister of state during the tenth century, this immortal was a student of Taoist magic whose three-legged toad could carry him wherever he wished to go. Several interesting legends associated with these characters imply that men's attraction to money may be their ruin but *Chan's* frequently seen image clenching a string of coins in his mouth make people associate him with luck in money. The coins on the string have also been associated with levels of examinations passed and therefore success.

The Fish

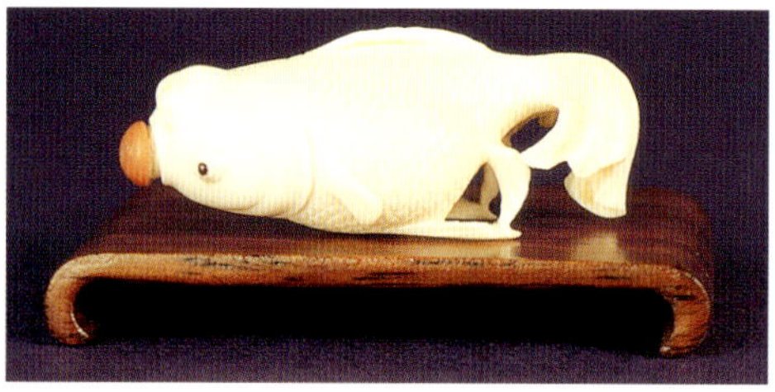

Singly or in pairs fish are associated with wealth and abundance as well as harmony and union. The word "*yu*" meaning fish also means remainder, suggesting that two fish would give plenty remaining beyond one's needs. The Chinese image of the two fish would normally be swimming in the same direction unlike the Western image of Pisces. The sight of a large carp rather than an ordinary fish would be a delight to a merchant or business man since it would symbolize big profit. The sight of a large carp in a lake was seen as a good omen. Little surprise then that a wealthy merchant would create a pond in his garden filled with healthy specimens.

The Lotus

One of The Eight Buddhist Emblems, the lotus has double importance in Chinese symbolism since it is viewed by Buddhists to be as important as the cross is to Christians. Hence the meditation position adopted in Buddhism is known as the Lotus. It is also linked with Taoism where it signifies fruitfulness and as a symbol of purity rising through the water from the rotting mud beneath. In different contexts the three generations of the lotus, that is, the bud, the flower, and the seedpod represent the past, the present, and the future. Use of these symbols in conjunction with others may well imply a time context for the recipient.

The Bamboo

Fast growing and extremely durable as well as upright, the bamboo is used to represent a person who is respectable. When seen alongside the panda it is obviously a life source and can also be used in association with other symbols of longevity.

The Peach

An accoutrement of the Taoist Immortal *Shou Lao* along with his knotty staff, the peach is linked with immortality. It is frequently a gift and a symbol associated with birthdays. Much of Chinese legend is associated with magical people or fairies, one of whom is described as The Fairy Peach. The Chinese believed that anyone who ate the peach attained immortality. The reader may also remember the legend of the Monkey King who stole the Peach of Immortality and as a result was ostracized from heaven.

The Gourd

Not only is the gourd a symbol used in Chinese decoration, the gourd itself was and is decorated in its own right. The ability to grow a gourd within a mold so that its soft flesh took on the appropriate shape allowed the artist immense flexibility. Thus the use of the gourd as the body of a bottle implied fertility and longevity but could be extended greatly according to the shape desired by the artist. However, unlike a carved glass bottle or an inside painted one, time was not on the artist's side, so a basic selection of shapes and symbolic impressions would have been essential.

Clear and green glass gourd shaped bottle with a waist band of green stylized petals. *Courtesy of Skippen Collection*. £40-60. $55-85

Clear bottle with a green carved fish curled beneath and up two facets of its body. *Courtesy of Skippen Collection*. £50-60. $70-85

Clear and amethyst glass depicting a pond with floating weed and tadpoles. Some water decoration to the inner bottle. *Courtesy of Skippen Collection*. £50-60. $70-85

Chapter Three: Glass

As this would appear to have been the first group of bottles to be made specifically for the purpose, it is only right that an analysis of glass bottles should begin here. They were clearly around in 1710 and probably long before that, but the way in which they were created is not as one might expect.

The Chinese regarded glass as a form of stone, transformed from sand by firing. The technique of rolling or blowing glass was not known in the early days of glass production in China. Instead, glass, once formed, was worked very much like stone with methods of grinding and cutting being employed to produce blocks or ingots of glass. With this limited technology glass working was a slow process and the price reflected the time and labor involved. The Chinese treatment of it as a semi-precious stone continued even after the introduction of other working methods, and it was not until about 1890 that it became relatively inexpensive. Throughout most of this period it was the lapidaries or stone polishers who did most of the structural work on the bottles before handing them over to decorators.

Not until the arrival of foreign expertise did Chinese artisans begin to blow glass and use molds. The production of glass therefore became less labor intensive. Blown glass can often be distinguished from carved glass by examination of the base of the bottle. Fine streaks of glass pulled together towards a center of the base or foot are usually indicative of a blown glass bottle.

The introduction of color into glass was achieved by the addition of various metallic oxides to the molten material. The background knowledge for this came from the long Chinese history of porcelain making and decoration which had long explored the use of oxides fired beneath a glaze to produce lavish colors. The Emperor Qianlong particularly favored an opaque yellow color, known as Imperial yellow. Obviously not all snuff bottles we see today of this color are Imperial in origin but throughout his reign it was forbidden for anyone other than the Emperor to own it. In later years, when the ruling was more relaxed, some other artisans began to use it but it remains a rare and much sought after color. In China it has a much less romantic name, being referred to as Chicken Fat or Chicken Oil Yellow.

A quirk of Chinese glass is that it usually contained a high degree of barium compared to other glass from around the world, making it

Unusual amber glass bottle with handle shoulders suitable for some form of carrying cord. *Courtesy of Skippen Collection.* £75-100. $107-145

Amber glass carved in form of a Buddha head. *Courtesy of Skippen Collection.* £60-80. $85-115

Carved amethyst glass with lotus petal decoration. *Courtesy of Penny Collection*. £60-80. $85-115

Small dark green glass bottle simulating fine colored jade. Probably late nineteenth century, 1.25" (3 cm). *Courtesy of Penny Collection*. £150-200. $215-285

Beautifully simple amber glass bottle showing slight signs of wear which suggests late nineteenth or early twentieth century origins. £80-100. $115-145

easily identifiable with chemical testing. However, as the vast majority of snuff bottles are Chinese it is not their origin but their age which comes into question and this is also a difference between the early and the modern pieces which rarely have the barium content.

Early glass snuff bottles were very alkaline and decomposition may occur within the material over time. This decomposition manifests itself as a network of fine fractures beneath the surface but is not absolute proof that the bottle is of any significant age. Nevertheless, the resulting pattern is highly sought after by collectors presumably because it gives them an indication that an item might be original. Known as "*crizzling*," this progressive deterioration does not appear as much in snuff bottles as larger pieces.

Carved Glass

During the reign of the Emperor Kangxi, in the late seventeenth century, a German Jesuit priest, Killian Stumpff, and his colleagues transformed glass working in China and gave birth to what we now call *Peking Glass*. This term is usually used to refer to the carved or cameo variety but this is not correct since many early pieces and their later replicas are of single color. Although they are clearly lacking in some areas, Forbidden City archives only record examples of cameo glass during the Yongzhen and Qianlong reigns. Earlier examples are claimed, probably quite rightly, and outside the walls of the Palace this style of work has continued right up to the present day despite periods of being out of favor.

These German experts lived and worked in the workshops of the Forbidden City and developed or expanded the use of glass, forming vessels of varying sizes and styles. While lapidaries continued to work their own magic to produce the actual bottles, Stumpff and his fellows used the workshop in the Forbidden City to create wonderful objects to delight the Emperor. As the Imperial taste so strongly favored snuff bottles it was inevitable that they should be among the resulting works though no specific examples can be identified because of the lack of personal attribution referred to earlier.

Simple blue glass bottle with carved ribbing simulating basket-work. £60-80. $85-115

Simple ribbed amber glass bottle with elegant neck detail. £80-100. $115-145

Superbly carved amber glass fish with scale and fin detail. An open mouth holds a pearl shaped clear glass stopper. £100-150. $145-215

Dark green glass bottle with carved bamboo handle decoration hollowed to allow a fine silk cord to suspend bottle. Two small holes angled through the foot also allow the cord to pass beneath the bottle and keep it stable. A fine nineteenth century example. £250-300. $360-430

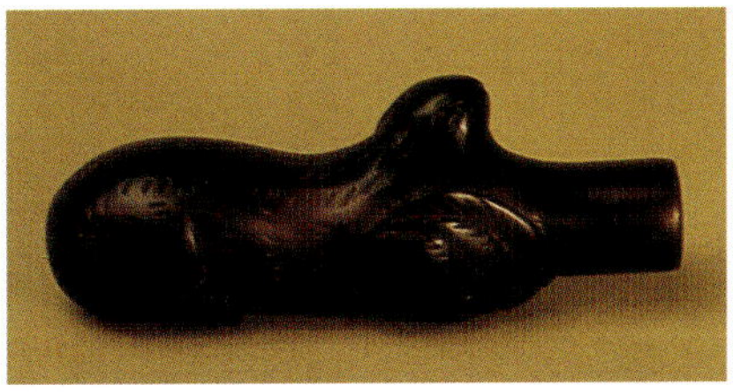

A tiny amethyst glass bottle carved in the form of a squirrel clinging to a branch. The squirrel's head is raised and the branch forms the neck of the bottle. 1.75" (4 cm) *Courtesy of Penny Collection*. £80-100. $115-145

Well-carved amber glass bottle in the form of a Chinese Buddha. £80-100. $115-145

Carved blue glass bottle resembling bamboo basket-work. £80-100. $115-145

Gourd-shaped milk glass bottle encased in silvered metal naturalistic filigree. £60-80. $85-115

Stylized carved amber glass lotus flower inverted so that the stem provides the neck of the bottle. £80-100. $115-145

Cobalt blue glass bottle infused with splashes of goldstone. £120-150. $175-215

A lovely simple Imperial yellow bottle of exquisite shape and tactile qualities. £150-200. $215-285

Simple carved pale amber glass in the form of a ribbed winter melon. £80-100. $115-145

Imperial yellow bottle in the form of a double fish. £80-100. $115-145

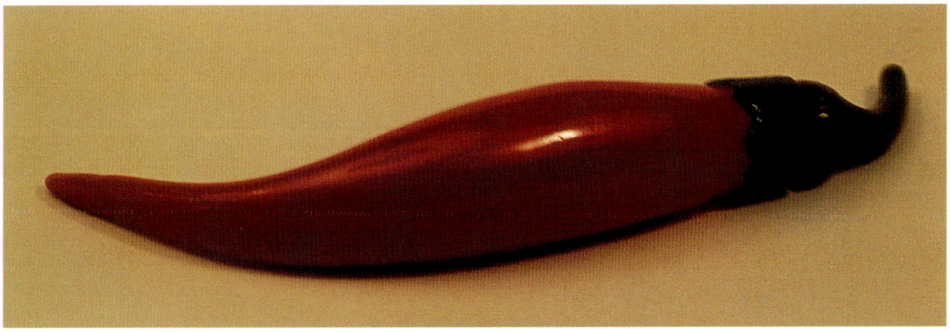

Beautifully executed red glass bottle in the form of a chilli pepper with green glass forming the neck and stopper as calyx and stalk, 4.5" (11 cm). *Courtesy of Penny Collection*. £80-100. $115-145

An amusing small Imperial yellow bottle carved in the form of a happy Buddha with a yellow glass hat style stopper. £130-150. $185-215

Rare clear bottle twisted with splashes of bright color. *Courtesy of Skippen Collection*. £100-150. $145-215

A yellow glass snuff bottle. Middle Qing dynasty, eighteenth century, 53 mm. (A) £800-1,200. $1145-1715

Superb dark amethyst glass bottle (appearing black) twisted with splashes of goldstone suspended in the glass. £150-200. $215-285

Twisted milk glass bottle in a naturalistic form incorporating *mille fiori* style splashes of color. Probably late nineteenth century. *Courtesy of Penny Collection*. £150-200. $215-285

Superb amber glass fish with suspended gold flecks. The fish is carved in excellent detail with the tail curled at the bottom and resting on an upwardly curved wave. *Courtesy of Penny Collection*. £200-300. $285-430

Above and right:
Superb milk glass bottle with red and green *mille fiori* style decoration twisted into the body. Signs of wear and style indicate nineteenth century origins. £150-200. $215-285

All five of these bottles have amber and black glass twisted over a milk glass inner bottle, not so that they can be cameo carved but so that the overall effect resembles tortoise shell. £100-120 each. $145-175 each

Superb carved twisted blue and white *mille fiori* bottle with lion head and ring detail to the shoulders. This rare bottle shows signs of wear and is almost certainly nineteenth century or earlier. £500-600. $715-860

Amber and black twisted bottle carved into a subtle and very tactile shape. Substantial wear and "*crizzling*" indicates that this is an early and well-loved bottle. *Courtesy of Klemer Collection*. £300-500. $430-715

A clear glass bottle twisted with yellow, green, and red splashes make this the owner's favorite bottle. Late nineteenth century? *Courtesy of Klemer Collection*. £150-200. $215-285

Very unusual bottle with an outer layer of green glass infused with gold leaf over an inner layer of turquoise glass. The exposed turquoise glass at the neck suggests that this bottle originally had a metal collar, probably gold, and almost certainly a matching stopper. Small areas of rubbing to the sides, shoulders, and foot indicate that it may also have been held in a metal framework. Eighteenth or nineteenth century. Foot detail shows the turquoise glass twisted with the green outer layer. £500-600. $715-860

A glass snuff bottle. Middle Qing dynasty, eighteenth century, 60 mm. (A) £500-750. $715-1075

Above and right:
Two excellent simulant bottles which would not look out of place or indeed feel out of place among agate examples which they copy. The warmth of the glass rather than the ice cold of the stone is one indication of their "treachery" as is the drawing together of the colors visible at the base of each. £120-150 each. $175-215 each

Simple pale green glass bottle simulating apple-green jade. £80-100. $115-145

Above and left:
The rich red color and mottled appearance might cause some to catalogue this as an agate bottle. Evidence to the contrary is in the form of slight mold marks along the sides and concentric rings formed by the colors of the glass around the neck. £60-80. $85-115

Continuous decoration in blue and white cameo around this bottle depicts a bird (probably a magpie) among flowering plants and rocks. *Courtesy of Skippen Collection.* £50-60. $70-85

An unusual blue and clear bottle depicting a bowl of flowers with the flowers engraved in *sgraffito* style rather than carved. *Courtesy of Skippen Collection.* £50-60. $70-85

Cameo or Overlay Glass

Cameo or overlay glass was one of the first overall types to become popular and remains so today. The basic bottle, be it carved, polished, blown or molded and which could be clear, colored, frosted or bubbled, was dipped in a glass of different color so that the outer layer eclipsed the inner. One or more further layers of color were then sometimes added before the cutting process began. The resulting single or multiple layered cameo effect was spectacular with the best carvers making full use of the differing thicknesses of each layer for their effects. Most bottles recorded prior to the middle of the eighteenth century are simple ones with just one overlay color but later examples record up to four outer skins. Archives from the Yongzhen reign record three types of glass in use which can be categorized as transparent, translucent and opaque and that these were made in fifteen colors as monochrome objects. Presumably the same colors were used for the overlays though not all may have been capable of working in this fashion. The details recorded are not totally clear and may refer only to the ingot colors worked by the lapidaries.

Since the term *Peking Cameo Glass* is so frequently used, it might be assumed that it was unique to the capital but much of this type is known to have come from Boshan in Shandong Province. Bottles from Boshan actually give us more insight into their makers than those from the Peking workshops where it was unheard of for individual artists to be recognized and for any dedication to appear other than one to the Emperor. Some of the Shandong makers by contrast signed with their own names, especially in later years, with the result that we still have records of them, albeit sketchy.

Two particular families in Shandong stand out for their work. Both, until recent years, were believed to have worked principally during the Qianlong era though evidence suggests that it may have been somewhat earlier. With little to go on other than their signatures on the work and the styles which they produced, it will no doubt remain a subject of debate for years to come. These two families, the *Yuan* and *Hsin*, produced work of superlative quality usually attributed to the Imperial workshops, and there is no doubt that bottles from their skilled hands lodged proudly among those in the Imperial collection. It is claimed that the color quality which they achieved owed its richness to the use of ground precious stones such as rubies and sapphires. Small dots of black carbon residue are frequently found in their and other provincial bottles from the ash in their small workshops.

Seal Type

From the middle of the nineteenth century onwards, a new group of cameo bottles began to emerge. They are sometimes referred to separately as "seal type" because, unlike most of their predecessors, they bore the seals of their makers. This shows a considerable liberalization of the control exercised by the Palace over such matters. Unfortunately there are few details of these craftsmen, but it is sufficient to say that the majority of such pieces are of high quality.

With all cameo glass bottles, of whatever period, it is the quality of craftsmanship which needs to be examined. Many bottles are crudely and clumsily decorated. In early examples this may be forgiven as the art was still being perfected, though the majority are of very fine quality indeed, but in later ones it is simply a sign of cheapness. Fine detail and skilled design shine out when the better bottles are held against their cruder companions. Of particular note are pieces which have further decoration added to the innermost layer of the bottle. This may be in the form of stylized waves or intricate patterns and is very difficult to achieve, as it must be cut in between the cameo decoration already completed. If plain, the smoothness of the inner surface becomes paramount as a sign of the quality of the finished product. Whether smooth or engraved, the inner surface can take longer to complete than what appears as the principle outer decoration.

Red over clear decoration with fish swimming in a pond with heart shaped floating weed and carved water decoration to the inner clear bottle. *Courtesy of Skippen Collection*. £60-80. $85-115

Blown and Molded Bottles

When blown and molded bottles took over from the cut and polished ones produced by the lapidary is difficult to establish but as late as 1770, long after their arrival, the Jesuits recorded that even though a great many bottles were being produced, "nothing was blown." It is also uncertain whether the locally produced glass ingots proved difficult to reheat and reform in the way that Europeans were used to. It may well have been necessary to import suitable glass or change the basic production methods before good results could be produced. It is equally possible, and even likely, that it was the Emperor's preference to use glass worked as though it were stone rather than follow new methods.

Complex Glass

Spurred on by successive Emperors' enthusiasm and demands to produce evermore complex and imaginative pieces, the craftsmen of China, both inside the Forbidden City and outside, rose to the challenge. This took them far beyond the basic dipping and carving of the cameo and non-cameo bottles and into using combinations of colors, ground stone pigment, stretching, blowing and chemical additives so that glass emulated stone and other precious materials and was so convincing that even today some bottles are incorrectly described. Agate and jade were popular stones to imitate, particularly the imported varieties of jade, since they were so highly sought after and expensive. Modern style faking for profit does not seem to have been the aim, however, so much as the expansion and expression of the glass workers' skills and their desire to please their ruler. In any case the qualities of natural stones like jade are such

Amethyst in clear glass crab decoration. *Courtesy of Skippen Collection*. £60-80. $85-115

A well-carved dark green and milk glass bottle in the form of a Chinese cabbage. *Courtesy of Skippen Collection*. £60-80. $85-115

Clear and amethyst (appearing black) with very simple decoration of the ancient *Pi* symbol on each side and a straight bar vertically on each shoulder. The *Pi* symbol is believed to represent the continuity of the universe. *Courtesy of Skippen Collection*. £60-80. $85-115

Simple miniature with clear inner bottle in amethyst glass outer carved as an open lotus flower, 1.25" (3 cm). *Courtesy of Penny Collection*. £40-50. $55-70

that it would be impossible to truly fake them. While the weight could be simulated by adding lead to the glass the coldness, hardness and specific gravity properties, particularly associated with jade remained beyond the glassworkers' art. In addition, glass is prone to the formation of tiny bubbles which should, to the keen and knowledgeable observer, give the game away. As has already been suggested, though, these imposters are a testimony to their creators' artistic drive and skill and hence do not appear among the fakes and forgeries of a later chapter.

Blended Glass

During the eighteenth century blended or polychrome glass bottles emerged, usually in opaque or translucent form. They are often likened to work emerging from Venice around the same period. Sadly a ship carrying a huge quantity of glass from the Emperor Kangxi to Pope Clement XI sank *en route* in 1721. Its contents were probably intended not just as a gift but a commendation of the quality of his own workshops. Snuff bottles undoubtedly formed a significant part of that shipment so they are a sad loss to our modern understanding of the subject.

With glass working being a constantly expanding and developing process, it is frequently difficult to date precisely the examples that are encountered. Research by collectors and museums has often resulted in changes to the way certain types of bottle have been viewed. With many early assessments of age being based upon reign marks and style it has often been said that a bottle is so complex it must be a late one. Complexity, on the other hand, seems to have been the hallmark of many early bottles with the recognition of simplicity and form coming later. Be that as it may, reign marks can rarely be verified unless a specific bottle has been recorded, so basic gut instinct seems to be as important to many collectors as anything else.

Gold Star Glass

One small group of bottles for which there are records are those known as "gold star" glass. Incorporating ground goldstone, which was occasionally used in solid form for bottles, in the glass these appeared in the late Kangxi era and lasted for about a century. Records for 1741 (sixth year of the Qianlong reign) show an order for sixteen of these bottles which took three months to make. The best effect is usually produced when the gold stars appear in darker colored glass. Later bottles of this type were made outside the Forbidden City.

Overlay Glass

Returning to the glass overlay bottle, as they are sometimes known, these are produced by dipping the plain glass body into molten glass of a differing color, thereby forming an outer coating with the dipped color. Once the outer coating has hardened, the artist sets about carving his design through the outer coating back to the original surface, leaving the design standing in relief in the contrasting color (cameo style). The technique did not originate in China since glass objects showing this overlay pattern have been observed much earlier in Egypt and Germany. The technique was almost certainly introduced by the Jesuits who may themselves have been imported for that very purpose. Cameo glass tributes from Europe would have made their way into the Emperor's hands and probably inspired him to seek the knowledge for his own craftsmen.

A variation on this method of decoration is the multi-colored but single layered cameo which always arouses great interest because of its apparent complexity. The technique is actually simpler than a dipped bottle because either blobs or strips of glass of color are applied to the outside and then carved in the normal way for a single layered bottle. Careful planning in the placing of the colors or imagination by the decorator result in very spectacular designs which are attractive and highly prized.

A full list of possible examples in glass, as in other materials, would be so diverse and extensive that it is impractical to show them all, but the examples illustrated should give the reader an idea of what to look for in order to create a comprehensive collection. However, be warned: whenever you think that you have every conceivable variation, a new one will come to your notice and rekindle the desire for more.

A five color overlay glass snuff bottle. Qing dynasty, nineteenth century, 65 mm. (A) £1,500-2,000. $2,145-2,860

Milk glass with red overlay in a vase shape depicting cranes both standing and in flight among clouds. *Courtesy of Penny Collection*. £50-60. $70-85

Clear and amethyst overlay finely carved with fish swimming in an exotic pond. £40-50. $55-70

A green clear octagonal faceted miniature, 1.5" (4 cm). *Courtesy of Penny Collection*. £50-60. $70-85

A milk glass inner bottle with overlaid dark green glass appearing black at the upper part where thickly carved and olive green in the lower where finely carved. £60-80. $85-115

Clear inner bottle thickly overlaid with red and crudely carved in the form of two fish. £30-40. $40-55

Delicately carved red decoration over a clear faceted bulbous bottle. £30-40. $40-55

A simple clear and blue glass overlay decorated with butterflies and clouds. £30-40. $40-55

A white and blue bottle depicting a traditional dragon. £30-40. $40-55

A clear and amethyst glass bottle carved in the shape of an aubergine with a large insect resting on it. The stalk stopper is missing. £50-60. $70-85

A clear bottle overlaid with blue and carved with a large flower, barred shoulders and separate foot. £50-60. $70-85

A rich blue bottle overlaid with white and carved to reveal a large flower head. £50-60. $70-85

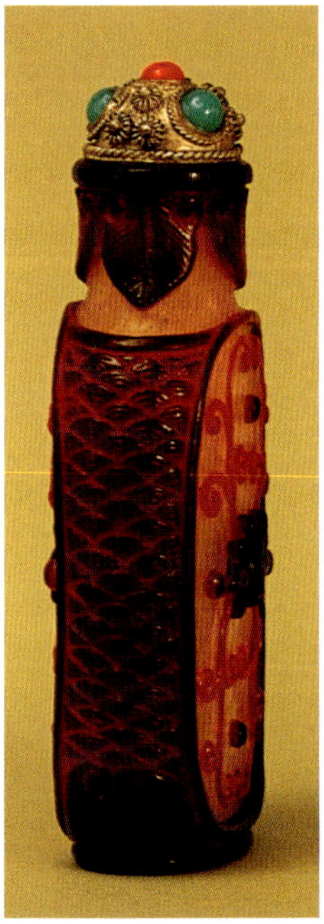

A mottled yellow inner bottle is thickly overlaid with red and then carved back to different thicknesses allowing varying depths of color to the red layer. Stylized lotus flower and tendril decoration with elaborate wave decoration to the bottle sides. £150-160. $215-230

An apparent leaf motif decorates this opaque white and blue glass bottle. £50-60. $70-85

A mottled four-sided clear bottle is thickly overlaid with amethyst glass appearing black in the bamboo detail and paler for the chrysanthemum. £80-100. $115-145

Clear glass bottle overlaid with green carved to reveal side handles and two simple green panels. Beautifully simple and effective. *Courtesy of Penny Collection*. £60-80. $85-115

Clear inner bottle with green overlay carved on one side with birds on a branch beneath gourds and a rose on the reverse. £50-60. $70-85

Exquisite detail highlights this opaque blue bottle overlaid with white and carved to depict a pond with carp and lotus and subtle wave decoration to the inner blue layer. The reverse shows two swans beneath the moon. £150-160. $215-230

A simple clear bottle overlaid with blue and depicting a fish among pond weed. £30-40. $40-55

Two bottles with red overlay show the effects of different types of inner layer. £40-50. $55-70

A blue dragon curls angrily around this opaque white bottle. *Courtesy of Klemer Collection*. £40-50. $55-70

A stork and a crane share this clear and blue bottle with unusual beaded decoration to the shoulders and sides. £40-50. $55-70

The decoration on these two clear and amethyst bottles suggests they are by the same carver. Each depicts fantailed fish in a pond and uses beaded shoulder decoration. £40-50. $55-70

A very unusual color combination makes this bottle stand out in a crowd. With a densely opaque inner layer of terracotta followed by layers of white and green this is a highly effective piece. £150-160. $215-230

A clear bottle with inner rippled decoration is overlaid with blue and shows a frog leaping into a pond. £40-50. $55-70

A blue crab is highlighted against the rippled effect carved into this clear bottle. £40-50. $55-70

Two clear bottles with engraved wave decorations are decorated with red overlay and similarly carved goldfish. £50-60 each. $70-85 each

This large cabinet bottle is magnificent in its simplicity with a complex repetitive basket-ware decoration over the bulk of its surface carved into the thick amethyst glass outer layer over the clear inner. £120-140. $175-200

A small bulbous bottle in opaque white overlaid with dark green and carved with images of fish and birds. *Courtesy of Klemer Collection*. £40-50. $55-70

The continuous landscape on this small white bottle depicts birds among rocks and sparsely blossoming branches carved into an outer layer of brown glass which is an unusual choice of color. *Courtesy of Klemer Collection*. £50-60. $70-85

A striking red and white bottle depicting blossoming branches. *Courtesy of Klemer Collection.* £40-50. $55-70

A ripe head of maize is delicately represented in this two color bottle. £40-50. $55-70

A simple two layer bottle with insects delicately carved in the outer red. *Courtesy of Skippen Collection*. £30-40. $40-55

A cleverly decorated opaque white bottle with a thin layer of red overlay. The central feature on each side is a bat which is echoed by two bats on each shoulder. Surrounding the bats are stylized representations of the character for long life which have been joined together at the top and used to thread a small string of cash. The overall symbolism is simple, long life, wealth, and good luck. A small amount of rubbing on this bottle suggests some age. £100-120. $145-175

A clear glass bottle overlaid thickly with green and decorated simply in the form of two discs and elongated ribbing to the shoulders. £40-50. $55-70

Two pale green stylized dragons twist and turn on each side of this simple bottle. £30-40. $40-55

Finely carved bottle with amethyst over clear glass depicting a dragon among clouds. £40-50. $55-70

A simple two-color bottle with crickets and Chinese cabbage leaves. £30-40. $40-55

Fine detail lifts this simple bottle above others of its kind. The three fantailed fish swim towards one another and the stylized water has been given ripples in the appropriate directions. £50-60. $70-85

The feathery fronds of a fern or palm tree are beautifully executed in a fan shape for this green and clear bottle. The simple effective decoration is delightful. £50-60. $70-85

An unusual two-layered octagonal bottle in clear and amethyst glass depicting on both sides a pair of mandarin ducks as a symbol of fidelity. £50-60. $70-85

The curl of the animal's tail in this two-layered bottle provides a ring through which this bottle can be hung on a cord. The detail of the legs, head, and tail highlighted by the dark amethyst outer layer are very pleasing. £50-60. $70-85

A rare green overlay snuff bottle. Qing dynasty, nineteenth century, 7.1 cm (2.75"). (A) £2,100. $3005

A ruby red overlay glass snuff bottle. Middle Qing dynasty, eighteenth century, 60 mm. (A) £1,200-1,600. $1720-2290

A carved red overlay glass snuff bottle. Middle Qing dynasty, eighteenth century, 60 mm. (A) £1,450. $2075

A carved red overlay glass snuff bottle. Middle Qing dynasty, eighteenth century, 57 mm. (A) £1,450. $2075

A three-layered bottle with a milk glass inner overlaid with red and then a further layer of milk glass beautifully carved with an array of butterflies. £100-120. $145-175

A carved red overlay glass snuff bottle. Middle Qing dynasty, eighteenth century, 53 mm. (A) £480-650. $690-930

A beautifully elegant milk glass bottle overlaid with green and highlighted with the use of an outer white layer depicting lotus leaves and flowers. £150-160. $215-230

A dark green inner bottle is overlaid with opaque white and red. The red is cleverly used to form a bird cage while the white forms the bird and other interior detail. *Courtesy of Penny Collection*. £150-160. $215-230

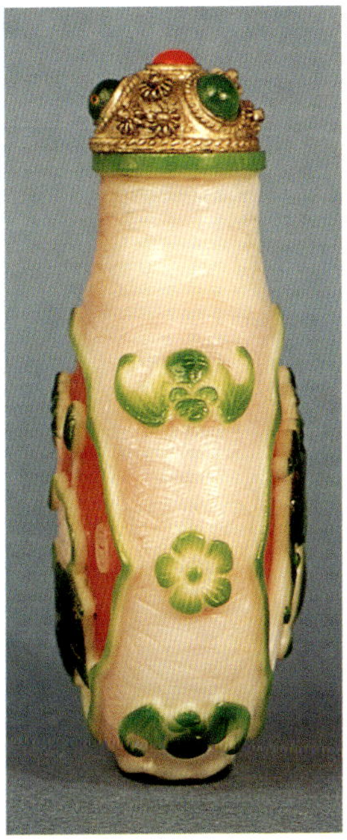

Opaque pink inner bottle overlaid with white and green carved with views through two decorative windows showing lotus leaves and flowers growing in bowls. Bat and flower decorations to side panels. *Courtesy of Penny Collection*. £150-160. $215-230

A gorgeously detailed three-layered bottle in a traditional style used for border decoration on the walls of important buildings. £150-160. $215-230

A cranberry inner bottle is overlaid with green and white and carved in beautiful detail depicting two of the Immortals. A Qianlong reign mark is featured along with an oval seal mark bearing the name *Jin Er*. The use in Chinese of "*Er*" in the name can have a double meaning indicating a second son. £150-160. $215-230

A three-layered bottle in opaque white amethyst and white highlighting it depicts cranes beneath the moon. A Qianlong style reign mark is featured along with a line of older style characters down one edge of the bottle. These characters read *Yu Sun Yue zhi* (made by *Yu Sun Yue*). £150-160. $215-230

Three-layered bottle with excellent carving depicting a continuous scene of a pond with lotus, carp, and fantailed goldfish. £150-160. $215-230

A fine three-layered bottle with green sandwiched cleverly between two layers of white. The outer layer of white has been carved back but remains over most of the green to soften the color. The overall effect is very pleasing. The subject is monkeys on a peach tree. £150-160. $215-230

With very good use of coloring this cranberry, green, and white bottle depicts two images of the famous Chinese warrior *Zhang Fei*, subject of several Chinese operas. A complex collection of seal marks read *"jie yang"* ("good luck" or "best wishes") on each side. Two circular seals read *"zheng"* (translated as "take care" but also common as a girl's name) and the other reads *"Zhang"* (the family name of the hero subject). A small square seal mark reads *"er"* (not a reference to the number "two" but probably part of the carver's name). The large oval seal reads *"xian zhang"* (like a god *Zhang*). As an important national hero whose image appears god-like as a guardian in many temples, these references would have wished success and a rise in rank to the recipient. £180-200. $260-285

A three-layered black and white bottle with what appears to be a seal mark. The beautifully carved subject depicts life on a lotus-covered lake with a sage being ferried by his servant and a fisherman sitting patiently. £150-160. $215-230

The unusual coloring of this three-layered bottle is used to striking effect. A layer of black between the inner white and outer green is used mostly for highlighting purposes. Cranes flying over a lush lotus pond form a typical Chinese scene. £140-150. $200-215

Both unusual coloring and choice of decoration set this bottle apart from most others. The inner light blue layer is overlaid with yellow and then black giving striking constrasts. The carved image then gives a complex series of symbolism with a celestial pagoda framed by a flying bat and crane and on the opposite side a stylized dragon stretching itself thinly through the center of a large cash or coin. *Courtesy of Klemer Collection*. £160-180. $230-260

This large magnificently carved table bottle has three layers of color. The inner mottled clear is overlaid with orange and then white and carved with an elaborate scene of the Buddha with three of his followers, 4.5" (11 cm). £200-300. $285-430

This three-layered bottle depicts scenes of tranquility with a fisherman on a lake with a pagoda in the background and a young man riding an ox and playing a flute. Excellent standard of carving. £150-160. $215-230

A beautifully carved three-layered bottle with two layers of opaque white sandwiching a layer of green. The continuous landscape depicts cranes flying and landing on a lily pond. Although the seal reads as a Qianlong reign mark it is done in a modern character form and is therefore not intended to deceive but simply to indicate the style origins of the bottle. £150-160. $215-230

A three color overlay glass snuff bottle. Middle Qing dynasty, eighteenth century, 45 mm. (A) £4,800-6,400. $6865-9155

An unusual color combination with milk white overlaid with yellow and then red giving an overall effect of orange. An apparent reign mark is clearly not an indication of its age. £100-120. $145-175

A complex four-sided seal type bottle with three layers of color. The inner yellow bottle is overlaid with dark red and opaque white used to maximum effect for highlighting. The four sides depict the seasons by the use of daffodils, monkeys picking peaches, water lilies and chrysanthemum. Two of the seal marks are in the form of an old style stamp (but not a word character) used by a shop to indicate good luck or as a logo. The third seal is simply "*nian*" or "year" without being specific. £120-140. $175-200

A complex three-layered seal type bottle with eight individual seals. On each side is a Qianlong style mark and also a seal depicting "*xiong*" (translated as "old brother") which is probably the carver's name. Additional oval motifs read "*jie nian*" ("good year") and "*gu wan*" ("antique" used on small items). A reverse character, white on blue, reads "*jie wang*" ("good luck") and a tiny circular seal reads "*hao*" probably an additional reference to the carver's name. The decoration itself depicts a warrior on his horse on one side and his attendant walking beside a horse on the opposite. £150-160. $215-230

This lovely red and white three-layered bottle appears orange with the clever carving and use of shade. It depicts an image of water birds beneath lotus leaves and flowers. Though appearing to be a reign mark the large seal reads "*Zhou Kai Xiu zhi*". "*Zhou*" is the family name, "*Kai Xiu*" the given names of the carver and "*zhi*" simply means "made by". An additional small seal mark reading "*ming*" is not a reference to the dynasty but translates as "famous". This may be a reference to the carver or more likely a wish that the recipient become famous. £150-160. $215-230

This mottled clear bottle has been overlaid by several colors in sections rather than layers. Use of yellow, green, red, blue, and black create a striking effect and make bottles of this kind very desirable. The scene is a simple one of a lily pond with ducks and butterflies. *Courtesy of Klemer Collection*. £150-160. $215-230

This complex small bottle has an inner layer of opaque white overlaid with dark green, appearing black, and then with splashes of red and yellow applied. The careful carving makes the bottle appear to have four layers because in places the green is carved thinly and can be seen as its true color. £60-80. $85-115

An unusual five color overlay glass snuff bottle. Qing dynasty, nineteenth century, 60 mm. (A) £4,800. $6,865

An unusual four color overlay glass snuff bottle. Middle Qing dynasty, eighteenth century, 60 mm. (A) £3,850. $5,505

A rare four-layered cameo bottle superbly executed with an inner mottled clear bottle overlaid with red, white, and green. Although different in appearance the signatures on each side of the bottle are the same reading "*Zhou Kai Xiu zhi*" meaning "made by a member of the *Zhou* family". £180-200. $260-285

An unusual bottle with an inner layer of twisted colors including amber and white. An overview of the neck of the bottle indicates the twisting colors. The inner bottle has then been overlaid with a dark amethyst glass appearing black. The overall effect is of an agate bottle carved to enhance a dark feature. The ferocious lion dogs which decorate it are well carved. *Courtesy of Penny Collection.* £100-120. $145-175

A very interesting cameo bottle with twisted glass in various shades of brown and cream with an outer dark layer intended to resemble an agate bottle. The way in which the carving is done also cleverly resembles an agate with a naturally forming silhouette. *Courtesy of Aisingioro Collection*. £150-200. *Photo by Ma Jun*. $215-285

Chapter Four: Natural Stone

The art of stone carving or polishing is by no means uniquely Chinese but it is safe to say that they have taken it to a level rarely seen elsewhere. The sheer variety of different rocks available in such a large country may well have been a factor but the art form has been taken to perfection. Most of the better Chinese hotels and restaurants sport huge and complex stone carvings depicting hundreds of individually detailed charging horses, enormous baskets of flowers or mythical battle scenes executed in such enormous detail that they are breathtaking. The greatest effect is achieved by clever use of the natural colors in the rock strata for which the planning and preparation must be immense. With such large pieces the practical problems of movement, access and fine detail must also be a headache but not so with snuff bottles.

The mottled red appearance of this beautiful nephrite bottle enhances its natural pebble shape. Extremely tactile this delightful piece shows signs of slight wear and is probably nineteenth century. £150-200. $215-285

The creation of the snuff bottle as a "canvas" for the artist opened up a huge new market for the stone workers of China, though it was obviously necessary for them to miniaturize their ideas. The result is arguably the most tactile of the various types available and stone bottles offer endless variety in texture, color and finish. Most popular among Chinese collectors was, and still is, jade.

Jade Snuff Bottles

Jade has clearly been highly prized by the Chinese for thousands of years with ancient artifacts of amazing quality and beauty being found in most major burial sites. Symbolic of longevity, clarity, wisdom, equity and courage its use extends from everyday objects for Emperors to jewelry and amulets for people at all levels of society. The prices attached to many small pieces of this magical stone frequently astound Westerners whose customs and education do not include its appreciation. Place two items together, no larger than a small coin, and prospective buyers will ponder and debate for hours over the relative merits of each and probably arrive at hugely different prices for them. If there were a single group of criteria which could be set out for such pricing it would be useful and easy to pass on to others but this doesn't seem to be the case. Color and texture are obviously important, with "apple" green

A large pebble of mutton-fat jade has enabled the creation of this piece which is deeply carved with images of two bats, one of which is carrying a string of cash through the clouds. £60-80. $85-115

Bands of darker color highlight this beautiful goldstone bottle which has lion head and ring decoration to the shoulders. £100-120. $145-175

being highly popular, but extensive observation suggests that other criteria are more arbitrary and individual to seller and buyer. If the two agree on the relative merits of one of our two pieces then a sale is possible but otherwise the debate will rage for hours and neither will leave satisfied.

In the West specialists tend to differentiate between jade, jadeite, chalcedony and the various other stones which make up the jade family but the Chinese tend to group them together under the heading "*yu*", often also including pale agates. They are all technically different stones with different levels of hardness and other qualities. *Jade (Anness Publishing Limited, 1991)*, a superb reference on this minefield of a subject seems to take the Chinese view and combines a whole series of treatise on these various stones under the one general jade heading. While many of the properties of the various jades make them fairly easy to distinguish to a lapidary or gemologist the distinctions remain largely elusive to most people. Little wonder then that the general term, jade, is so widely used.

Jade actually consists of two distinctly different classes of minerals, jadeite and nephrite. Nephrite ("Spinach Jade") has been available to the Chinese since the Neolithic Era (3,500 B. C.) and is known as "Chinese Jade". The word jade comes from the Spanish "*piedra de ijada*" meaning "stone of the side". It was believed to alleviate pain on the side of the body where the kidneys are situated. Nephrite, on the other hand, comes from the Latin *lapis nephriticus*, but still means stone of the kidney. Not only did the Chinese wear jade as a symbol of longevity, it became a talisman to ward off illness, harm and misfortune and was thus highly prized.

The word "*yu*", in Chinese, simply means a stone which can be carved, it does not refer to any of its other physical, structural or chemical properties. This broad inclusion seems to suit many western collectors who are less interested than their Chinese counterparts in the subtle nuances which might otherwise escalate the price. For those who may wish for a little more detail we have attempted a brief guide but the subject warrants extensive reading and, more importantly, a great deal of hands on experience for anyone to become an expert.

China has the world's largest resources of nephrite, which exists in a huge range of colors, most popular of which are white, yellow and pale green. It is generally opaque and creamy in appearance and has a soft waxy luster to the surface. Some soapstones may be mistaken for nephrite or jade in general but can easily be recognized be the fact that cut edges when scratched reveal a whitish powder. Nephrite, being much harder, is almost impossible to mark by simple scratching and leaves no white residue.

Jadeite appeared much later in China than the native nephrite and was not actually used there until approximately 1750, when it was imported from Burma. Jadeite is almost translucent with an "icy" crystalline structure which is often visible. It has a much more highly polished finish and a vitreous or glassy appearance. It is also slightly harder than nephrite and among the green jades, it has a more brilliant color than we find in green nephrite. Its brilliant apple green and emerald-green color tones are the most highly prized. Indeed, in terms of jewelry, jadeite in these colors is of gem quality and very expensive. A whole snuff bottle made from such a material would be very extravagant with a price tag to match. It is no wonder then that jadeite is referred to as "Jewel or Imperial Jade" by the Chinese. Jadeite may also appear in various shades of blue or lavender, not found in nephrite. Unlike their nephrite counterparts, jadeite snuff bottles generally show little or no carving, being able to rely on their natural color and beauty for effect. Jadeite and nephrite may be found intermixed in the same stratum of rock and are, therefore, easily mistaken for one another.

Snuff bottles purporting to be made of either jadeite or nephrite may, in fact, be made from a variety of other green colored stones such as aventurine quartz, chrysoprase or chalcedony. Agate also appears in a green form and pale varieties may be dyed green in the hope of imitating jade. This dying is also sometimes used in jadeite bottles to enhance their look and imitate the more valuable Burma jade. Poor quality attempts tend to be fairly obvious but only microscopic examination will reveal the truth in some cases. Some say that this is fakery but others argue that the craftsman has intentionally dyed the stone to enhance its beauty. On a similar theme, the blue stone, turquoise, can now be synthesized artificially and darkened to a more popular color. Does this then make the synthetic bottle with the perceived popular color more desirable than a faded natural turquoise bottle, or indeed, does it matter?

Lions head and ring motifs are the only embellishments on this beautiful early bottle. The dark areas in the stone make it appear to have been burnt in a fire. Its apparent, if not real, survival was ideal symbolism for someone triumphing over adversity. *Courtesy of Penny Collection*. £150-200. $215-285

Design and Decoration

However the materials are defined, it is the subtlety of design and decoration and their incredible tactile nature which makes this group of bottles so popular with collectors and can make them expensive. The artist's undoubted foresight in carving and polishing a bottle to such a precise shape or style of decoration that the natural colors are enhanced is remarkable and, indeed, it is this particular feature which is so sought after. In some illustrated examples a tiny speck of red or other color has been enhanced to become the main feature in the decoration of an entire bottle.

It is the creator's gift to the collector that he has seen and enhanced two small black spots in an otherwise pale stone and from them has created the eyes of a fan tailed carp, with its mouth hollowed out for the neck of the bottle, or slight streaks have given rise to the fins or tail of a mullet.

Such fine and subtle details have been the delight of generations of Emperors and snuff bottle collectors. The hollowing of the bottles until they are translucent and in some cases only one or two millimeters thick is a major feat in itself with flaws and layers in the stones always threatening fragmentation. Neck and foot details and often-carved lion heads and ring decoration on the shoulders simply add to the complexity of the work and the enjoyment of the end product.

Complex figure subjects, where the carver or polisher has used hats or other details to disguise the presence of the stopper, show the degree of thought and planning which has gone into them. With conventionally shaped bottles it is a distinct advantage to have the original stopper designed for the bottle, since it will probably be of the same material and color, but with the figures and similar bottles it is almost essential to get the full beauty of the design. With most other types of bottles it may be impossible and, frankly, irrelevant to know whether the stopper is original. Most glass bottles, for instance, were made with stone, coral, silver or gold tops but few of them had glass stoppers. Few stone bottles, however, appear to have been made with stoppers of other materials. Exceptions tend to have stoppers of another stone of contrasting color rather than a completely different material.

As with the cameo glass, already discussed, we tend to refer to the method of decoration as carving which wrongly implies some sort of whittling process involving a blade. Although this may be the case with softer materials such as soapstone it is totally incorrect for the hardstones. In many areas of China, particularly those close to the source of good stone, fine "carving" still goes on and it is possible for the visitor to watch the artist at work. Excellent workshops can be visited in Xian and Suzhou as well as other cities where the modern craftsman uses the same basic tools as have been worked for generations. The availability of electricity may have made the process a little less strenuous but the skill needed remains the same. Though the stone is much harder than the cameo glass and has many natural flaws, which can lead to fragmentation, the basic method of polishing is much the same.

Red inclusions appear vein-like in this nephrite pebble bottle. Probably nineteenth century. *Courtesy of Penny Collection.* £100-120. $145-175

Lapidary Artisans

Historically Suzhou seems to have been the principal lapidary center of China with the best artisans being encouraged or co-opted into the Imperial workshops in Beijing. Locals may disagree, but the Xian workshops were of much less significance until relatively recently with tourism undoubtedly playing a major part in their growth. The importance of Suzhou is highlighted by a poetic reference to its famous *Zhuanzhu* Lane by Emperor Qianlong himself. In it he spoke of the huge congregation of lapidaries and their endless striving for new designs and ideas. It was also said that the noise from the workshops disturbed the people living in the area.

The cutting tool is a little like a drill bit though with a ball like end of varying size and coarseness to create the fine or larger detail and polishing. The cutting or drilling tool is in a fixed place, though the angle may be variable, and it is the material being worked which is moved to and from the rapidly spinning bit. In the not too distant past, even late into the twentieth century, many workshops used treadle like machines, similar to sewing machines, with the artist using his foot to propel the tool. This mechanical version was an extension and development of the "pole lathe" used in both East and West for centuries to decorate wood and other materials. In that instance the wood was turned and the blade held to it but the basic principle of operating the tool was much the same.

Extensive experience in jade and stone carving generally meant that with the arrival of the fashion for snuff bottles in the Imperial Court they were an obvious choice for a new market. The basic ideas were already established by the glass workshops so it was simply a matter of re-interpretation to transfer them into stone. However, it was not so easy because the need for a hollowed out container, and moreover one with a very narrow opening, was unfamiliar to the lapidaries. Looking closely at a good stone bottle of any kind will reveal how difficult it must be to work inside the shoulders of the bottle to imitate the outside shape in the hollowed area. Of course, it would be perfectly easy to produce a simple tube-like interior, and this may well be found in some cheaper bottles, but the craftsmen of China rose to the challenge and worked the stone so thin that it became translucent.

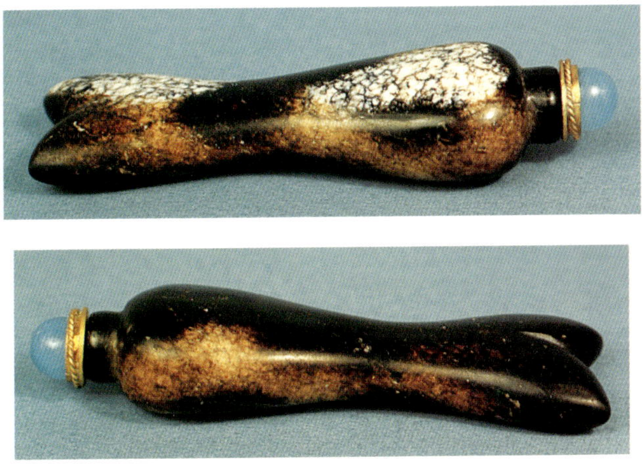

The mottled three-tone appearance of this dark chalcedony is enhanced by it being carved in the form of a fish. £80-100. $115-145

From an initial lump of plain stone must emerge an item of beauty through the skill and control of the craftsman's hands. It is a painstakingly slow process with no margin for error. A slight slip might remove an ear from an animal, a vital stroke from a calligraphic character or the petals of a tiny flower. So subtle is the detail and the importance of it in symbolic terms that such a slip would render an important work valueless. The buyer would be wise to examine stone bottles closely to avoid the accidental chips which may have made the piece, what we would call, a second or reject.

A dark green and white jasper bottle in squared form with original stopper. *Courtesy of Klemer Collection*. £50-60. $70-85

It is an indication of the time necessary for each bottle that in the third year of Emperor Qianlong's reign (1738) an order was placed for thirty-five bottles from the Imperial workshop which took two years to fulfill. Further records show that in 1767 some four hundred and thirty three pieces were submitted for Qianlong's approval by the workshops of Xinjiang of which only eight were considered first rate. It would appear that while the designs produced were of interest the workmanship fell short because orders were sent to Suzhou for bottles to be made in the same styles. Undoubtedly the Xinjiang standard would meet with most people's approval and it is this area which is famous for its "pebble" jade bottles, many of which are from stones found in the riverbeds.

Quartz

Quartz can be divided into two main groups of minerals, namely crystalline quartz and cryptocrystalline quartz. Crystalline quartz is more or less transparent whereas cryptocrystalline quartz is generally opaque. Rock crystal, amethyst, smoky quartz, hair crystal and rose quartz are all members of the crystalline quartz group. Chalcedony, agate, jasper, carnelian, bloodstone and onyx belong to the cryptocrystalline group. It is the impurities in both groups which produce the myriad of colors seen in quartz.

Many snuff bottles made of quartz have little carving in them, rather the artist has let the natural colors speak for themselves. Indeed, a region of color or an imperfection in the quartz may be cleverly integrated in the overall design of the bottle. The master Chinese craftsman will often carve without predetermined design. Amazingly, we are told, they can see the picture of the completed bottle in their mind's eye and work towards its completion, often without the possibility of correction, even though the layers of color cannot be seen in the stone until the outer layers have been carved away.

As mentioned earlier, it is the impurities in quartz which produce its many colors. Rock crystal however, is free from all coloring matter and as such may look like glass. The relative rarity and difficulty in carving meant that only the wealthy could afford rock crystal and it was extremely lavish to have one made into a snuff bottle. Late in his reign the Emperor Kangxi is recorded as having given a rock crystal bottle to an envoy of the Pope who was visiting from Rome. Some rock crystal snuff bottles have also been used for inside painting as well as being intricately carved. Unlike glass, rock crystal will not scratch and is highly favored by the Chinese as a symbol of purity. Some rock crystal may contain needle-like inclusions of rutile or tourmaline which are like very fine strands of hair within the structure of the stone. For obvious reasons these are known as hair crystal and snuff bottles carved out of it are much sought after. The variations in density of the "hair" fragments and their color are such that they have been the entire focus of some collectors' attention though they are very rare to find and early examples with provenance are highly expensive. Particularly attractive are those with, what looks like, strands of gold running through them, which are actually titanium dioxide.

Other types of quartz crystal snuff bottles include smoky quartz, rose quartz, amethyst, chalcedony, jasper, agate, aventurine quartz and crocidolite (Tiger's Eye) quartz. Though carved decoration may be seen in some instances it is usually the natural features of the stone, enhanced by a simple shape, which give these bottles their unique appeal.

A simplistic image of a cicada forms the body of this bottle which is very tactile and easily carried. The ball-like stopper suggests that the insect is carrying a black pearl. Both are symbols of good luck and prosperity. *Courtesy of Klemer Collection*. £100-120. $145-175

The soft pink color of rose quartz is due to titanium salts within the mineral. Snuff bottles made out of rose quartz should be kept out of sunlight as the light and heat may cause the color to fade.

The purple to deep magenta color associated with amethyst is due to manganese oxide in its substance. It is the deep purple color and the flawlessness of the crystal which is most desired by collectors. Heat and light may also cause loss of color so it is important that amethyst snuff bottles are kept away from hot and bright places. Amethyst was highly prized in Imperial China but now cheaper imports, mainly from Brazil, have reduced the price of new materials. Despite this amethyst snuff bottles remain relatively rare and expensive because the highly flawed structure of the crystal makes it very vulnerable to fragmentation when hollowed out. There is, therefore, much less risk attached to producing items other than snuff bottles. In addition the best pieces of amethyst, those with rich and unflawed color, attract a much higher price in the jewelry market where a piece of the size necessary for a snuff bottle will make many brooches or rings.

This very dark flat circular chalcedony bottle is very tactile and easily accommodated in a narrow pocket. Probably nineteenth century or earlier. *Courtesy of Penny Collection*. £100-120. $145-175

Chalcedony appears in many colors and is moderately translucent with a waxy luster. Bloodstone, carnelian (otherwise known as cornelian), chrysoprase, "moss agate" are all forms of chalcedony. The mineral has been used extensively in the manufacture of snuff bottles, as it is reasonably inexpensive as a raw material. Moss agate and dark green jasper are both frequently referred to as "spinach jade".

Jasper is actually a variety of quartz which is dense and opaque in appearance and contains various metallic compounds within its substance.

Agate belongs to the cryptocrystalline quartz group and is admired for its banded patterns. Agate snuff bottles usually have little or no carving on them, the artist generally preferring to let the natural beauty of the agate bands speak for themselves. Where carving does exist it tends to be of a type which makes best use of the contrast banding to create a cameo effect.

Aventurine quartz, otherwise known as quartzite appears in a host of colors, one of which is known as goldstone which is reddish brown with what seem to be specks of glittering gold, but are inclusions of iron oxides, within its substance. It may also appear in a spangled

Simple shallow relief carving of a ribbon and cash is the only embellishment necessary on this lovely lapis lazuli bottle which probably dates from the end of the Qing dynasty. *Courtesy of Klemer Collection*. £300-400. $430-575

green or dark blue form due to deposits of chrome mica. It has frequently been used to great effect in ground form melted with glass.

Tiger's Eye (crocidolite) is quartz with inclusions of asbestos which produces a reflective appearance to the mineral. Best known for its use in modern jewelry it has long been considered to have healing and other qualities. Few snuff bottles are seen in Tiger's Eye but those which are tend to be especially attractive. It was a popular stone for larger cabinet or table bottles and often appears in the form of a tortoise or turtle because of the resemblance of the stone to their shells.

Puddingstone Agate

Puddingstone agate snuff bottles are conglomerates of sedimentary rocks cemented into a compact mass by chalcedony or some other quartz mineral. The cementing substance is a complex mixture of carbonates, silica, calcium salts and clay.

Conglomerates of volcanic rock, cinders, ash and stone fragments are termed amygdaloidal basalt. A small number of snuff bottles have been carved out of both amygdaloidal basalt and puddingstone agate and can be very attractive though difficult to truly identify.

Semi-precious Stones

Snuff bottles made of semi-precious stones such as lapis lazuli and malachite were made in the late nineteenth and twentieth centuries, towards the end of the Qing dynasty. Such bottles are rare since the cost of the materials could not usually be justified for the making of an entire object but would normally be used as small inlays or decorations in another material. In the same way as many old gold snuff bottles would have been melted down long ago once snuff fell out of fashion or as times became hard so too would many semi-precious stones have been re-worked for more economically viable use.

With workmanship and attention to detail such as this, there is little wonder that many collectors look for nothing other than Chinese artifacts, whether they are snuff bottles or other products and irrespective of their age. A customer commented recently that he had been an avid collector of porcelain figures, by a well-known British company, but had switched his allegiance totally once he had handled Chinese stone carvings. He said that it was the uniqueness and tactile nature of the pieces which "spoke" to him.

For this very reason we have left this and other groups of bottles to speak for themselves through the photographs, enhancing them, where necessary, with additional detail. There is, however, no substitute for the experience of handling them and admiring the work of both the Divine and craftsman creator.

An unusual black jade bottle carved in relief on one side with a panel containing a bridge over a river between two cliffs overhung by a tree. *Courtesy of Klemer Collection*. £200-300. $285-430

Bottles of this quality are rarely seen and even more rarely available to purchase. The blue one is carved from a single piece of lapis lazuli and has a stopper in agate carved in the form of a bird but also intended to be viewed as a calyx and stem. The green jade bottle is a very rich color and is carved in the form of a winter melon with leaves and blossom and has a turquoise stopper doubling as calyx and stem but in an animal form. *Courtesy of Aisingioro Collection. Photo by Ma Jun*. £900-1,000 each. $1,290-1,430

A rare carved tourmaline snuff bottle. Middle Qing dynasty, eighteenth century, 52 mm. (A) £7,000. $10,010

A carved tourmaline snuff bottle. Qing dynasty, nineteenth century, 47 mm. (A) £2,400. $3,435

The very complex banding of this large agate pebble has been enhanced by it being carved in the form of a tortoise with a centipede and other insects and a frog and a snake on its back. The removable head forms the stopper. £120-150. $175-215

Careful polishing has revealed a dark area in this agate bottle which resembles a duck. Such bottles were considered lucky and are indeed rare. The opposite side of the bottle might even be considered to show the duck's eggs. £200-250. $285-360

Careful examination of this bottle reveals the jelly-like areas towards the base which make this bottle more interesting than most other agate examples. £180-200. $260-285

An extremely beautifully carved pale agate bottle in the form of a circle of bamboo with high shoulder handles and a contrast agate stopper. Lightly cut into either side is the double-happiness character surrounded by a design similar to the Greek key pattern. £350-400. $500-575

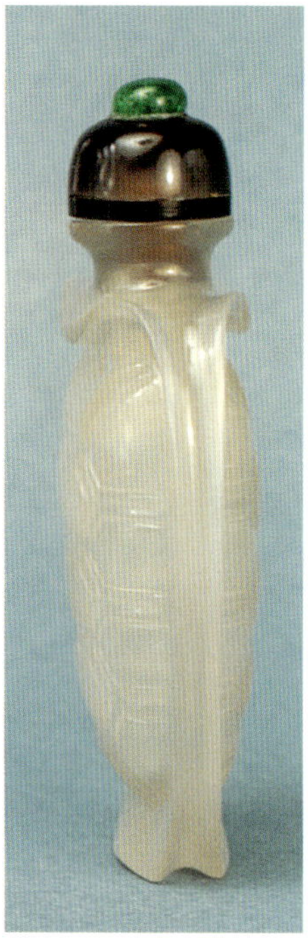

A superbly elegant pale agate bottle resembling white jadeite in the shape resembling a turtle shell and with appropriate decoration. The shell-like carving is echoed on both sides and has a shallow valley around the shoulders and to the base. The stopper which appears to be original is of dark smoky quartz and darker green jadeite. £800-1000. $1,145-1,430

The many layers of color in this amazing agate bottle have inspired the carver to produce this unusual table piece. The goddess *Guanyin* relaxes upon a white lotus leaf upon the back of a crouching elephant. Beside the goddess' foot is a black frog which forms the stopper of the bottle. *Courtesy of Penny Collection*. £400-500. $575-715

The simple elegance of this beautiful white and gray agate bottle makes it this collector's firm favorite. The finely carved shoulder rings and integral loops remain intact as does the matching stopper. *Courtesy of Penny Collection*. £300-400. $430-575

Small areas of black in this otherwise white agate (resembling jadeite) figure of the Buddha have been highlighted as bats. The bat resting upon his head forms the separate stopper. *Courtesy of Penny Collection*. £300-400. $430-575

A beautifully marked moss agate bottle with a tiny red inclusion which gives the observer the idea of looking into a pond full of floating weed. The red stopper matches well the small inclusion. £150-200. $215-285

No embellishment is necessary for the superb banding in this agate bottle where the colors range from white to dark red. £100-120. $145-175

A tiny white and pale pink nephrite bottle. Probably nineteenth century and perhaps color-enhanced but nevertheless very unusual and rare, 1.3" (3.2 cm). *Courtesy of Penny Collection*. £150-200. $215-285

The elegant colored banding of this agate bottle needed no embellishment but has nevertheless been given mock lion and ring handles to the shoulders. £100-120. $145-175

Bright yellow and orange agate make this a vibrant bottle upon which children are playing around a rock upon which sits a very large lotus leaf. A small dark inclusion has been cleverly used as the body of a dragonfly. Unfortunately no stopper exists for this bottle so we are unsure what the carver intended should sit above the rock. £200-250. $285-360

An elegant pale agate bottle cleverly carved so that slightly darker areas highlight the edges. The tall elegant neck has a carved collar with lion and mock ring handles to either side and the original two-colored stopper above. £300-400. $430-575

An extremely pretty white agate resembling jadeite with linen-fold style decoration and ribbon handles revealing three rings on each side and a darker brown contrast stopper. £300-400. $430-575

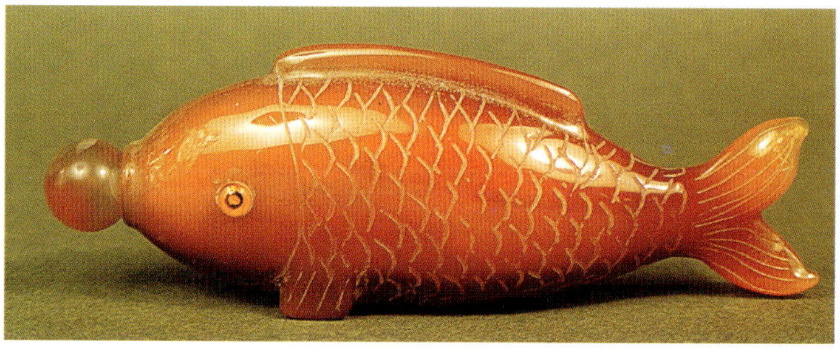

A rich red banded agate bottle carved in the form of a fish with an agate bubble in its mouth as the stopper. £80-100. $115-145

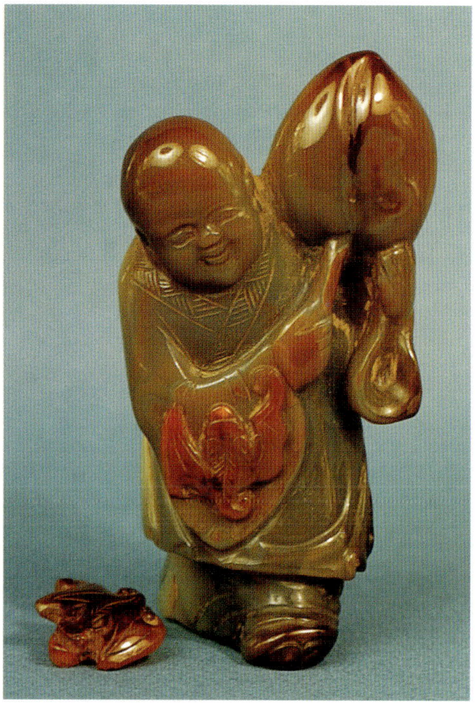

A humorously carved figure of a boy carrying a peach larger than his head on its stalk and with a bat clinging to the sleeve of his robe. A second bat sits on the back of his head as the stopper. £150-200. $215-285

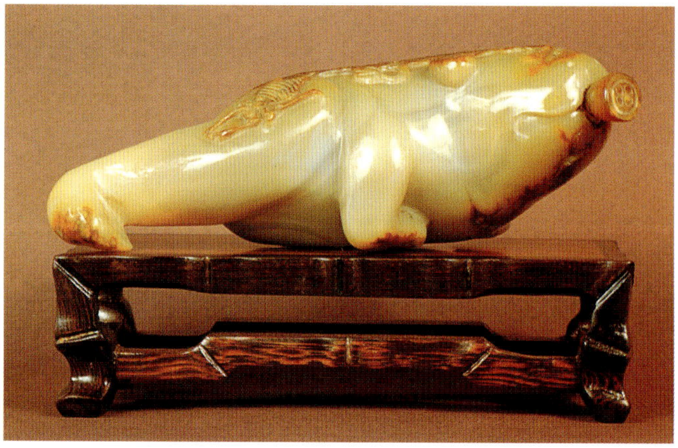

A large green and brown agate table bottle in the form of a four-legged toad. Carved onto its back are a scorpion, a centipede, a snake, another toad, and a spider. The stopper held in its mouth is in the form of a lotus pod, 6.0" (14 cm). £250-300. $360-430

A sturdy banded agate bottle. £50-60. $70-85

The clever carving of this piece of agate to reveal its bands along the side of the bottle make it very desirable and rare. The dark reddish-brown area on one side is in stark contrast to the paler bands immediately behind it. £200-250. $285-360

This Siamese-twin bottle shows a whole range of vibrant colors which make agate bottles so collectible. Double-bottles in any material are rare. £150-200. $215-285

Opaque white patches enhance the appearance and decorative qualities of this lovely bottle with simple lion's head and mock ring handles to the shoulders. £120-140. $175-200

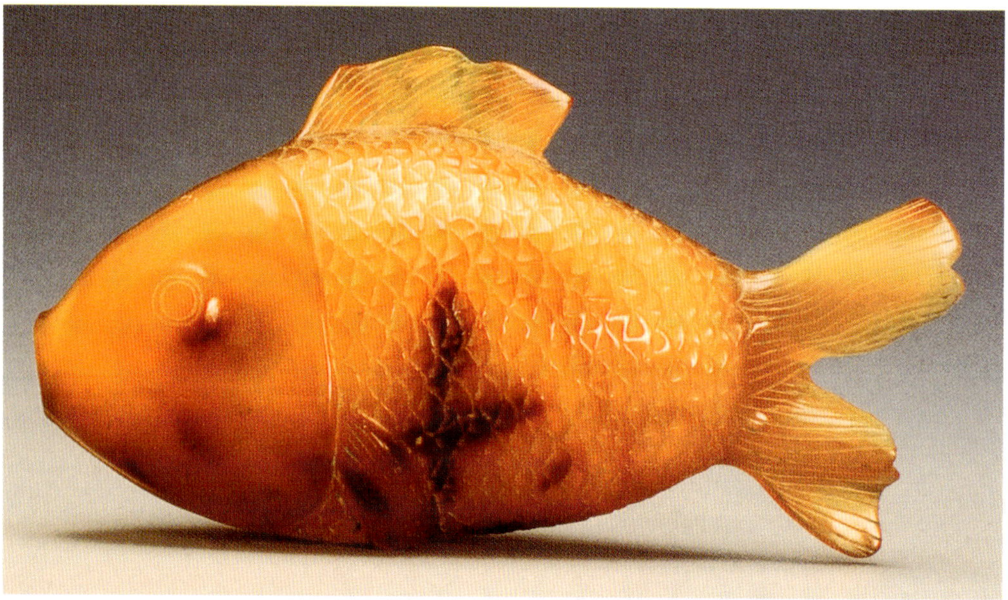

A rare and finely carved agate fish shaped snuff bottle. Qing dynasty, nineteenth century, 118 by 68 mm. (A) £1,720. $2,460

A very rare Imperial agate snuff bottle. Seal mark and period of Qianlong (1736-1795), 47 mm. (A) £14,350. $20,520

Left and below:
A rare carved agate snuff bottle. Middle Qing dynasty, eighteenth century, 60 mm. (A) £5,750. $8,225

An algae agate snuff bottle. Qing dynasty, nineteenth century, 54 mm. (A) £1,450. $2,075

A finely banded agate snuff bottle. Qing dynasty, nineteenth century, 60 mm. (A) £2,200-2,500. $3,150-3,575

A rare and finely carved agate snuff bottle. Middle Qing dynasty, eighteenth century, 7.2 by 6.3 cm (3 by 2.5"). (A) £6,500. $9,295

A very rare smoky quartz crystal bottle with fitted cover, ring handles to bottle and cover and chain threaded through the hole in the style of a Japanese *inro*. The stopper and two matching beads are in amethyst and the whole is threaded onto a silver chain. The authors are not aware of any other bottle in this style. £1000-1200. $1,430-1,720

A lovely hair crystal bottle with a white jadeite stopper. The simplicity of shape is enhanced by the careful polishing of the bottle to reveal the spray of golden hair-like inclusions. £400-500. $575-715

A small smoky quartz bottle carved on both sides with an image of a teacher and his pupil. £80-100. $115-145

An elaborately carved bottle in the form of a mythical cross between a tortoise and a lion. The superb carving and detail is highlighted by the use of the curled back tail as the stopper. £400-500. $575-715

A simple bottle in which the fragmentation of the amethyst crystal is its principal decoration. £120-150. $175-215

A simple vase shaped rock crystal bottle which features inclusions of orange-red. £120-150. $175-215

A lovely clear rock crystal bottle carved as an asymmetrical gourd entwined with branches and leaves threaded with cash. *Courtesy of Klemer Collection.* £150-200. $215-285

A large rock crystal table bottle in the form of a jar being held up by three boys. The jar itself is entwined with lotus stems and leaves and has its original stopper. Crystal bottles of this size are very rare, 3.75" (9.0 cm). £400-500. $575-715

A dark gray nephrite bottle with small areas of the more familiar pale green. This simple old bottle is similar in form to many medicine bottles. £60-80. $85-115

Gray white with black inclusions make this tiny nephrite bottle unusual but not highly desirable, 1.25" (3 cm). *Courtesy of Penny Collection*. £50-60. $70-85

A clear rock crystal bottle carved in the form of a double gourd and entwined by vines full of smaller ones. *Courtesy of Aisingioro Collection. Photo by Ma Jun.* £900-1,000. $1,290-1,430

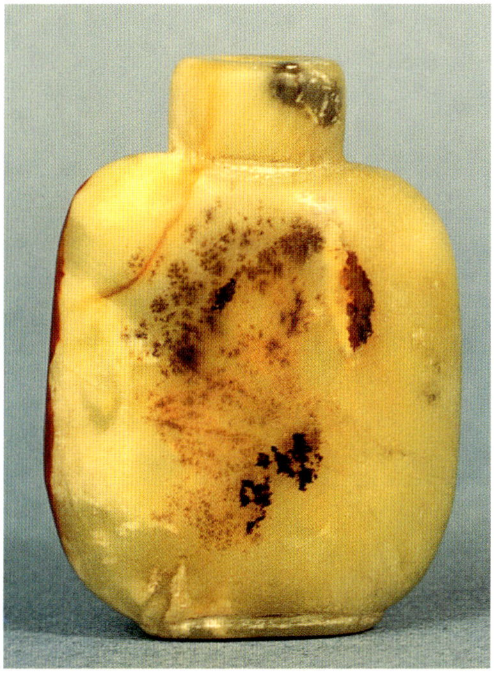

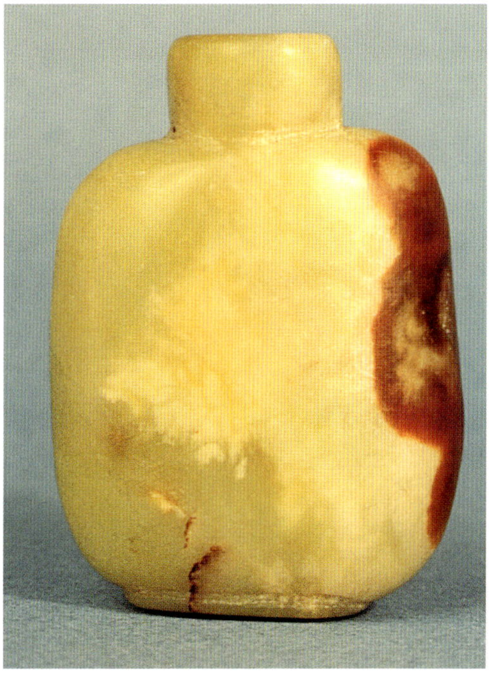

Areas of red and brown in this green nephrite bottle make it a prized example of a simple bottle where the material is decorative in its own right. Probably nineteenth century. *Courtesy of Penny Collection*. £150-200. $215-285

A beautiful but simple white jade pebble with red vein-like inclusions. Probably nineteenth century or earlier with inconclusive provenance. £300-400. $430-575b

A very flat dark green jasper bottle showing signs of regular use. Probably eighteenth or nineteenth century. £200-300. $285-430

A white jade snuff bottle. Middle Qing dynasty, eighteenth century, 69 mm. (A) £1,900. $2,720

Known as finger citron this fruit is considered lucky because it resembles the Buddha's hand. In this instance it is carved in a mottled green chalcedony with the original stopper. £100-150. $145-215

A fine white jade snuff bottle. Middle Qing dynasty, eighteenth century, 71 mm. (A) £1,200-1,600. $1,720-2,290

A white jade snuff bottle. Middle Qing dynasty, eighteenth century, 68 mm. (A) £1,000-1,500. $1,430-2,145

A jadeite snuff bottle. Qing dynasty, nineteenth century, 81 mm. (A) £3,900-4,300. $3,905-4,305

A finely carved yellow jade gourd shaped snuff bottle. Middle Qing dynasty, eighteenth century, 66 mm. (A) £3,000-3,900. $4,290-5,580

A very simple white nephrite bottle with original stopper. Probably nineteenth century. £100-120. $145-175

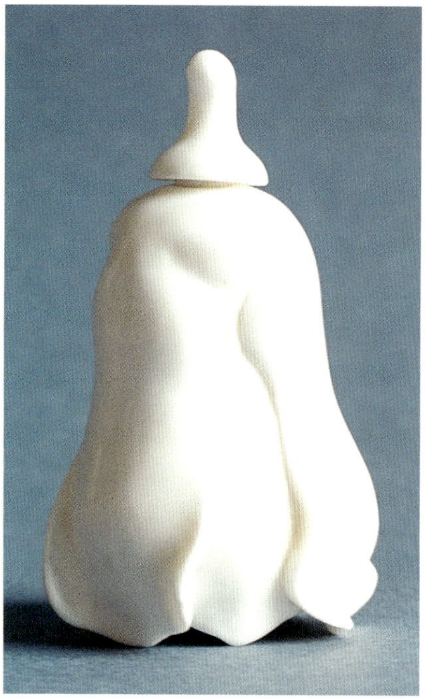

A beautiful white nephrite bottle in the form of an inverted Chinese cabbage. £180-200. $260-285

An olive green and brown-tinged nephrite bottle in the shape of a gourd with an integral waist ring. *Courtesy of Penny Collection*. £120-150. $175-215

A small apple-green nephrite bottle of squat proportions with original stopper. The evenness of the color would suggest that it has been enhanced. *Courtesy of Penny Collection*. £120-150. $175-215

The choice of a pale green and brown nephrite is deliberate in this vase shaped bottle with decoration reminiscent of archaic pottery. The simplistic pattern is slightly engraved into the surface and rubbed to appear worn with age. The overall effect is charming especially as it has its original stopper. *Courtesy of Klemer Collection*. £150-200. $215-285

An extremely unusual double reticulated pale green nephrite bottle with both upper and lower rings highly pierced and indicative of the quality of workmanship needed. *Courtesy of Klemer Collection*. £150-200. $215-285

Two stylized dragons climb the shoulders of this pale green jadeite bottle. *Courtesy of Klemer Collection*. £100-120. $145-175

Above:
It is almost impossible to do justice to the workmanship which created this fine piece of jadeite. The flattened water carrier shape is enhanced by the integral shoulder rings and chain. The delicacy of the carving and its survival intact make it a rare item. The single character carved into the bottle itself reads "*shou*" ("long life"). *Courtesy of Klemer Collection*. £800-1000. $1,145-1,430

A red nephrite bottle shaped and carved to resemble an archaic bronze. *Courtesy of Penny Collection*. £80-100. $115-145

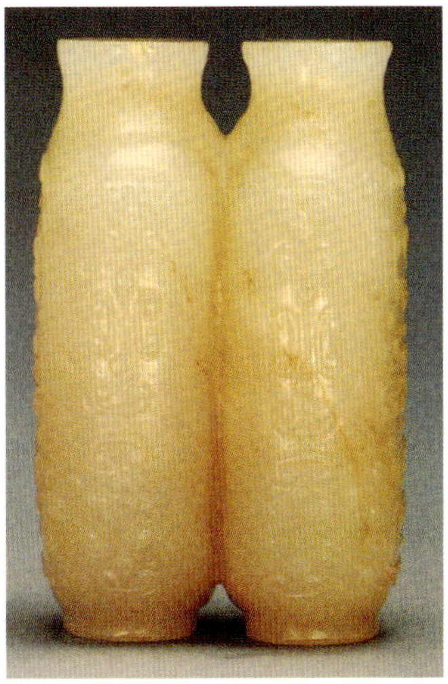

A finely carved celadon jade "twin" snuff bottle. Mark and period of Qianlong (1736-1795), 42 mm. (A) £4,400. $6,300

A fine jade snuff bottle. Middle Qing dynasty, eighteenth century, 60 mm. (A) £2,400-3,200. $3,435-4,580

A finely carved celadon jade cock shaped snuff bottle. Middle Qing dynasty, eighteenth century, 64 mm. (A) £4,800-5,600. $6,865-8,010

A particularly fine white and green jadeite bottle, probably for table use, with exquisite carving enhancing the splashes of rich green. On one side coins or cash are strung on a vine and on the reverse a dragon curls into a figure eight. Additional detail high on the shoulders leaves two small holes suitable for fine silk cords but the bottle seems too large to be of the carrying type, 4.5" (10.5 cm). *Courtesy of Penny Collection*. £500-600. $715-860

A gorgeous pale green jadeite bottle embellished with the relief carving of a boy returning from the fields on the back of a buffalo followed by the farmer. *Courtesy of Klemer Collection*. £250-300. $360-430

A somewhat crudely carved pale green nephrite bottle with a scene of someone being viewed through a window sitting beneath a tree. The reverse of the bottle is plain and the shoulders decorated with mock ring handles. A well-matched coral stopper enhances its appearance. *Courtesy of Klemer Collection*. £200-250. $285-360

The exquisite relief carving on this white and green jadeite bottle is incredibly detailed. Two lion dogs are playing with a ball among vegetation whilst a baby lion dog sits on top of the bottle as its stopper. Tiny double ring holes on each shoulder suggests that the bottle is intended to hang on fine silk cord. *Courtesy of Klemer Collection*. £450-500. $645-715

A rich mottled green jadeite with fine ring handles to the shoulders and extensive carving in the form of a vine with gourds. Original stopper. *Courtesy of Klemer Collection*. £300-400. $430-575

The keen eyed observer would note that the area around the mouth of this fish is damaged. Sadly this happened immediately after purchase but the bottle remains an important part of this collection. Surprisingly, with the contrast in colors between the red and the white this is a natural jadeite piece with the subject carved to enhance the natural flow of the colors. Such a piece carved in the West would undoubtedly merit a signature but unfortunately no credit can be given to a specific carver. *Courtesy of Klemer Collection*. £800-1000 (undamaged). $1,145-1,430

A white and green jadeite pebble carved in high relief with an image of a dragon carrying a vine strung with cash on one side and two stags beneath trees on the reverse. Other complex symbolism suggests that this is an important bottle. The tiny stopper is original and appears to be carved in the form of a bat. £500-700. $715-1,000

This large and very handsome jadeite bottle would form an important part of any collection. The mixed colors including a splash of brown enhance its appearance. The decoration is a series of individual motifs including mythical tortoise, peach, lotus leaf, and dragon. Tiny shoulder rings are unlikely to be intended to carry the weight of this heavy bottle, 4.25" (11 cm). £600-700. $860-1,000

A very excellent carved black and white jade snuff bottle. Middle Qing dynasty, eighteenth century, 76 mm. (A) £28,700. $41,045

Chapter 5: Porcelain

Porcelain bottles were probably the earliest containers used for snuff. Some writers suggest that they may have been adapted from previously made perfume bottles and miniature vases. However, as we have already suggested it is much more likely that they developed from the small medicine bottles which already existed and were predominantly made of porcelain.

Porcelain is made from a mixture of china clay, known as kaolin, and white china stone, known as petuntse, to produce a glaze which, when fired to a temperature above 1,280 degrees centigrade, produces a vitrified and impermeable substance of extreme hardness. The Chinese were the first to create true porcelain which eluded their European competitors for several more centuries. It was this which made Chinese porcelain a sought after commodity among the wealthy and fashion conscious of London, Paris and other European cities.

Genuine porcelain is distinguished from earthenware in that it is very resistant to scratching and shows a natural whiteness and translucency. It should also emit a musical note when struck. Unlike earthenware, it is non-porous and when chipped should show brilliantly white throughout its substance. Of course, to ascertain whether your snuff bottle is truly made of porcelain, damaging it would not be an option.

Various types of porcelain bottles have been produced. Some have been enameled, made to look like other materials, under-glazed and painted, or glazed without design. A small number of bottles may also be reticulated, where the bottle is made in several parts which move separately, but must be fired as one piece because it is impossible to assemble them afterwards. These bottles really do show off the skill of the artist that made them because, apart from the different elements of the bottle being independently moveable, they are usually intricately molded, pierced , or with a lattice of open spaces superimposed upon a solid bottle beneath. The outer bottle is purely decorative surrounding the inner one which is the container for the snuff. This is a very demanding technique as the firing process must be just right to allow the two bottles to form without cracking or, more likely, fusing together.

These porcelain bottles have been hand painted with enamels over the glaze and then refired. The quality of the workmanship is surprisingly good for the market at which they have been aimed. The subjects are stories from Chinese history and mythology and reflect ideas of morals and personal status. Prices do vary but should be buyable between £30 and £50, $40-70. Lower quality imitations may have applied transfers or very poor quality painting and can be purchased for as little as £5, $7. However, once compared with the better quality versions they will have little interest for most collectors.

The first bottles made specifically for snuff and for Imperial use were recorded in the Kangxi period, though none of these are believed to remain in the Forbidden City collection. This belief is based upon the styles attributed to that period though ongoing research may change opinions. Porcelain bottles throughout the Qing Dynasty which were ordered for the Emperor were made in Jingdezhen, the long-established center for porcelain production and development. Here there were two distinct groups of kilns, those devoted to official production and the local ones which concentrated on the home and export markets. Their production was by no means limited to snuff bottles, in fact, they formed a very small proportion of the overall output but warranted a disproportionate amount of time to make. The vast majority of the output was domestic style vessels such as bowls, plates, cups and decorative objects such as figures. The Imperial Court alone accounted for around 10,000 vessels or pieces per year.

Once again we refer to the records of *Zaobanchu* to discover that Emperor Qianlong ordered that only fifty bottles be produced each year and that these should be without stoppers. These would have been added later in another material by the workshops in the Palace. On another occasion he sent a vase to Jingdezhen ordering that forty bottles be made to the same design. At the time it was winter and the kilns were closed but it was unheard of to disobey the Emperor so the workers were brought together, the kilns opened and the batch completed.

As with so many other porcelain products the most popular throughout the Qing Dynasty were the blue and white while limited numbers were made with the red (iron oxide) under-glaze decoration or with over-glaze enamels. Decorations were as varied as in any other material and developed over time as the expertise grew in working on this small scale.

In addition to the Jingdezhen kilns those of Guangzhou (Canton) were also put to good use as the snuff bottle culture and fashion grew. While the porcelain was not considered to be as good, and there do not appear to have been any official workshops there, the local "*famille rose*" style decoration suited this small scale of working and some of this city's output undoubtedly reached the Imperial collection in the form of tributes and gifts. Much of the output from Guangzhou was of bottles imported from Jingdezhen unglazed and then painted and finished locally. These bottles were referred to as "*yancai*" (foreign color) which is often mistaken by collectors and dealers for "*sancai*" (three color) and "*wucai*" (five color). As these terms are usually used in connection with decorative styles of earlier dynasties it is often implied that such bottles must pre-date the actual arrival of snuff in China or that they are in imitation of an earlier style.

In the vying for status between the cities, pieces of all kinds would have been sent in the hope of attracting attention and official recognition, not to mention substantial orders, and the special interest given to snuff bottles would not have gone unnoticed. However, despite all efforts the majority of the output from Guangzhou remained for the general commercial market. Unfortunately for them, despite the popularity of their general product in Europe, the snuff bottle never took the place of the snuffbox in this other potentially lucrative market.

An exquisitely delicate mountain landscape decorates this vase shaped bottle. The decoration is with finely applied enamels. £60-80. $85-115

A rather worn and well-used green and white bottle with simple decoration which may have started life as a container for medicines. £30-40. $40-55

This small simple bottle, probably made in the nineteenth century, has delightful decoration. The enameled portrait of one of the Eighteen Lohan with very elongated eyebrows is of excellent quality, while the bowl and incense on the reverse is in simple contrast, 1.5" (4 cm). £60-80. $85-115

Cylindrical white porcelain bottle in the late Qing period with a charming figure of a man in under-glaze and over-glaze decoration. Slight chip to base. *Courtesy of Li, Jin, and Yan Collection. Photo by Ma Jun*. £300-400. $430-575

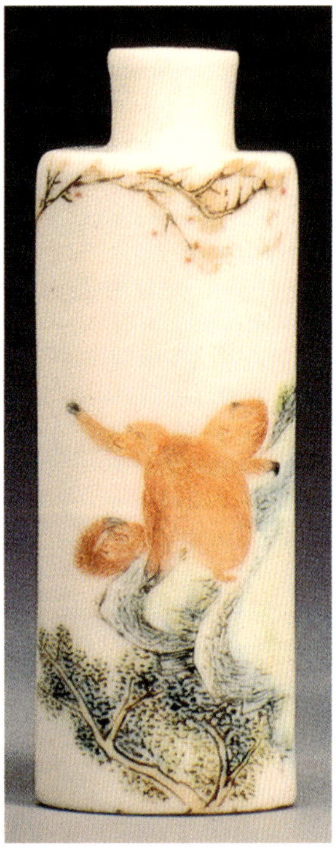

A *famille rose* porcelain snuff bottle. Qing dynasty Daoguang (1821-1850), 74 mm. (A) £1,000-1,200. $1,430-1,720

A fine *famille rose* porcelain snuff bottle. Seal mark and period of Jiaqing (1796-1820), 68 mm. (A) £1,000-1,200. $1,430-1,720

A molded *famille rose* porcelain snuff bottle. Mark and period of Qianlong (1736-1795), 75 mm. (A) £2,400-3,200. $3,435-4,580

A molded *famille rose* porcelain snuff bottle. Mark and period of Qianlong (1736-1795), 69 mm. (A) £1,200-1,600. $1,720-2,290

European style decoration is here seen at its best. Inspired by an earlier example, neither the original creator nor the later decorator is likely to have visited Europe and so will have extracted the idea from engravings or examples of European porcelain. The back panel showing branches of a pine tree with a squirrel is also probably intended to appear European but has a distinctly oriental flavor. Additional embellishments to the enameling of this bottle are lavish and highlighted in gold. £250-300. $360-430

The initial shape of this cicada-shaped bottle will have been molded, but the fine detail has been carved into the biscuit after initial firing. Painted and glazed in dark red, it has then been highlighted with delicate touches of gold. One eye removes to reveal the interior of the bottle. £200-300. $285-430

A beautifully decorated under-glaze and over-glaze enamel bottle depicting a warrior on a horse. This Chinese opera type character is racing through the countryside to get to his lover before an older suitor can tempt her with his barrow full of wares. The base of this bottle bears the reign mark "*Jia Qing Nian Zi*" but is not of that period. £200-250. $285-360

An extremely complicated double reticulated bottle lavishly decorated in bright enamels. The inner cylinder is enclosed by two independently moveable outer bottles and each has been separately painted. The base bears a "*Dao Guang*" reign mark in acknowledgement of the period of its inspiration. £250-300. $360-430

A beautifully enameled bottle in the Cantonese style with *famille rose* colors depicting a scene in a palace or important household. This one has a "*Jia Qing*" style reign mark. £200-250. $285-360

A cleverly modeled porcelain bottle depicting a boy, climbing a peach tree, suspended over a lake of lotus, collecting a coin or cash from the three-legged toad *Chan*. The image of *Chan* is unusual in that his single leg is shown at the front instead of at the rear, as is normal. The whole bottle is richly enameled in *famille verte* colors and gilded. £200-250. $285-360

This carved porcelain bottle is beautifully enameled with an image of a warrior in full armor mounted on his horse on one side and his attendant walking beside the horse on the reverse. Golden lion heads decorations appear in relief on the shoulders and the bottle is generally enhanced with gold decorations. £200-250. $285-360

Rich yellow and red enameling decorates the relief tracery on the side panels of this exquisite bottle. The front and back window panels are decorated with images of a bird and a cricket among flowers. The whole is richly gilded. A Qianlong reign mark indicates the origins of the bottle in this style. *Courtesy of Penny Collection*. £200-250. $285-360

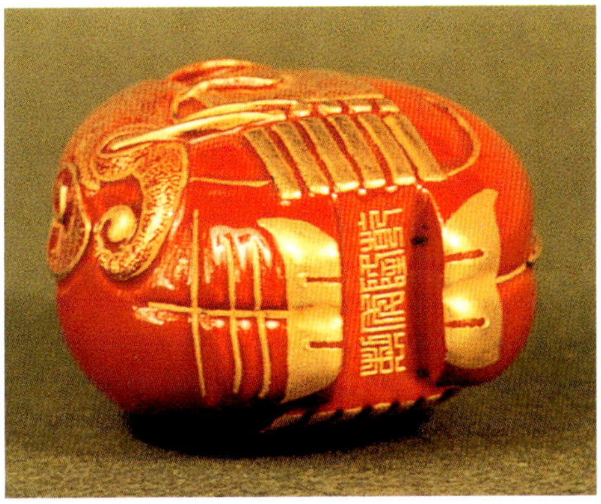

A beautifully molded and carved porcelain elephant has been richly decorated in red enamel enhanced with gold. A replica Qianlong mark appears beneath. £200-250. $285-360

A wide bodied vase shaped bottle in relief carved porcelain with fan shaped window panels showing birds on a bamboo stalk and a pomegranate tree. The side decoration in enameled relief shows bats flying among clouds and cash. A blue Qianlong reign mark decorates the base. £200-250. $285-360

An exceptionally Imperial porcelain snuff bottle. Seal mark and period of Qianlong (1736-1795), 54 mm. (A) Estimated at £20,000-28,000. Achieved £49,750. $71,145

A fine and rare *famille rose* porcelain snuff bottle. Qing dynasty Daoguang (1821-1850), 77 mm. (A) £5,750. $8,225

A porcelain snuff bottle. Seal mark and period of Qianlong (1736-1795), 6.3 cm (2.5"). (A) £1,475. $2,110

A porcelain snuff bottle. Seal mark and period of Qianlong (1736-1795), 6.0 cm (2.25"). (A) £2,400. $3,435

A superb reticulated porcelain bottle with cobalt blue decoration in between the piercing. Extraordinarily, the inner bottle around which the outer pierced one moves, is also painted. As the bottle cannot be constructed after firing, this is an unusual feature and requires great skill. £150-200. $215-285

Delicate under-glaze blue painting would be typical of larger versions of this vase shaped bottle. On such a small scale this style does not always appear balanced but in this case is highly successful. £40-50. $55-70

A beautifully decorated blue and white bottle with handles from neck to shoulder and molded relief detail. £100-150. $145-215

Delicately molded detail is highlighted by the use of a slightly green (celadon) glaze which appears white when thinly covering the relief areas and darker when filling recesses, as at the base. The brush work of the blue decoration is very free-flowing and attractive. £50-60. $70-85

An elegant bottle with unusually elaborate use of cobalt and iron-red decoration. Two scholars stand beneath a tree probably debating the relative merits of their pupils. £50-60. $70-85

A simple blue and white bottle with splashes of iron oxide which have been unsuccessfully fired and show brown rather than red. An old bottle from a small workshop, this is a good example of the affordability of some of the earlier pieces. £40-50. $55-70

Above and right:
A beautifully decorated "*mei ping*" vase shaped bottle with a typical lid acting as the stopper. The excellent under-glaze blue decoration is all applied by hand and is very good quality. The three character mark on the base is not a reign mark but reads "*yu chun tang*" ("jade spring place") which is probably the name of the workshop. *Courtesy of Klemer Collection*. £120-150. $175-215

A blue and white porcelain reticulated bottle with heart shaped piercing. The painting depicts children celebrating the Lantern festival. A Qianlong reign mark appears on the base. *Courtesy of Klemer Collection.* £120-150. $175-215

A large late Qing table bottle from around 1880 with under-glaze blue and iron-red decoration in a typical high shouldered vase shape, 5. 0" (12.5 cm). *Courtesy of Li, Jin, and Yan Collection. Photo by Ma Jun.* £1,100-1,200. $1,575-1,720

Three similar bottles in cylindrical shape each decorated in cobalt blue with a carefully controlled crackle glaze. The delicate painting shows the care taken even with some of the less expensive bottles. £50-60 each. $70-85 each

A vase shaped porcelain bottle with cobalt blue decorated carved relief areas around an olive green and brown painted body, late nineteenth century. *Courtesy of Li, Jin, and Yan Collection. Photo by Ma Jun.* £200-250. $285-360

Two nineteenth century vase shaped bottles showing completely different decoration. One has a complex pattern in under-glaze cobalt blue and under-glaze iron-red, and the other has a network of fine deliberately introduced crackles in the glaze highlighting the blue and white porcelain in the unaffected areas. Slight chip to one bottle. *Courtesy of Li, Jin, and Yan Collection. Photo by Ma Jun.* £300-350 each. $430-500

Two cylindrical white porcelain bottles from the nineteenth century both with under-glaze iron-red decoration. *Courtesy of Li, Jin, and Yan Collection. Photo by Ma Jun.* £250-300 each. $360-430

A large white porcelain table bottle painted with a cobalt blue dragon on each side. This mid to late twentieth century bottle could easily be mistaken for an earlier version but is of sufficient merit to warrant a place in a good collection. *Courtesy of Li, Jin, and Yan Collection. Photo by Ma Jun.* £80-100. $115-145

Three modern porcelain copies of earlier bottles all hand-painted and of good quality. *Courtesy of Li, Jin, and Yan Collection. Photo by Ma Jun.* £30-40 each. $40-55

Two modern bottles in white porcelain with different forms of decoration. The cylindrical bottle has a faint crackle glaze in the areas not painted with the underglaze blue dragon. The brown rimmed detail of the other bottle and its decoration are reminiscent of eighteenth century porcelain. *Courtesy of Li, Jin, and Yan Collection. Photo by Ma Jun.* £40-50 each. $55-70

A molded porcelain lotus leaf shaped snuff bottle. Qing dynasty Daoguang (1821-1850), 67 mm. (A) £1,000-1,200. $1,430-1,720

A blue and white porcelain snuff bottle. Mark and period of Daoguang (1821-1850), 66 mm. (A) £3,800. $5,435

A blue and white porcelain snuff bottle. Mark and period of Daoguang (1821-1850), 34 mm. (A) £1,700. $2,435

The decoration on this double figure porcelain bottle depicting a Mandarin and a lady is delicate and belies the price. Both figures are hollowed as bottles. £50-60. $70-85

Each of these reclining ladies has been carefully molded in porcelain and hand-decorated with under-glaze colors to produce a vibrant result. Each is holding an article to add to their elegance and also the difficulty of manufacture. As would be typical of such ladies, each has bound feet and it is one of these bound feet which must be removed as the stopper for the bottle. Rarely seen at all in this quality, even as modern bottles, it is unusual to encounter more than one. *Courtesy of Penny Collection*. £150-200 each. $215-285 each

A charming molded "tourist" bottle in the form of a child holding a cash and decorated in under-glaze blue. £25-30. $35-40

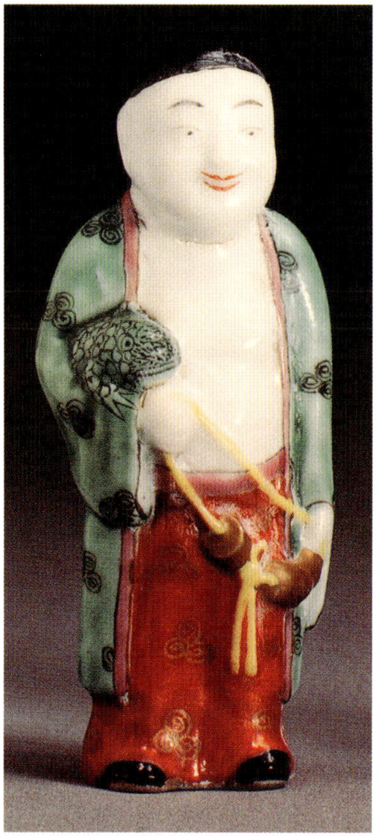

A *wucai* porcelain human shaped snuff bottle. Qing dynasty Daoguang (1821-1850), 90 mm. (A) £950. $1,360

A beautifully molded and enameled bottle depicting Pig (from the Monkey King legend) carrying a young woman (probably the princess) on his back. The bun of her hair forms the stopper. £40-50. $55-70

A fine *wucai* porcelain human shaped snuff bottle. Qing dynasty Daoguang (1821-1850), 77 mm. (A) £1,900. $2,720

Each of these bottles shows the same under-glaze technique sometimes referred to as "frost on a window pane". The random nature of this method of decoration and subtle use of color make them extremely attractive. Also sometimes referred to as a "virus" glaze because it spreads beneath the surface and continues to do so for sometime after firing. £50-60 each. $70-85

The highly pierced outer decoration hides an inner bottle on this delightful piece with turquoise-colored glaze. A fearsome group of lion dogs surround it, presumably to protect the contents. £80-100. $115-145

Two dark blue glazed nineteenth century medicine bottles of similar style. £30-40 each. $40-55

A molded bottle in the form of lion dog appearing to swallow a vase. Delicately enameled over the glaze and designed so that the bottle can lie flat or stand upright. £100-120. $145-175

A *Yue Hua You* porcelain snuff bottle. Qing dynasty Daoguang (1821-1850), 6.5 cm (2.5"). (A) £1,450. $2,075

A glazed ceramic bottle with yellow crackled finish. This bottle clearly has some age and is probably a simple early nineteenth century version. £120-150. $175-215

Partially glazed cream colored porcelain bottle in a double gourd shape resembling an item of archaic pottery. A Chinese export sticker has been left on this bottle as part of its charm. Probably nineteenth century. *Courtesy of Penny Collection*. £80-100. $115-145

A flattened ovoid copper bottle with richly colored *cloisonné* enamel decoration in a background of black. £50-60. $70-85

Chapter Six: Enamels

While enamels have been and still are used with materials such as glass and porcelain, it is those with a metal base bottle which are dealt with first in this chapter. The majority of these have a copper base though others in bronze, silver, and gold are known and can command very high prices. It is necessary to break down the groups of enameled bottles into several types based upon the technique used. Each of these has arrived in China from abroad and then been developed and integrated into the Chinese art forms familiar today.

The enamel itself is a mixture of flint or sand, red lead, and soda or potash. The opacity and color of the enamel is altered by the addition of coloring agents which are usually ground semi-precious stones. An enameled snuff bottle is usually made on a copper body to which enamel has been applied by one of the methods which follows. In some instances white enamel is applied, the piece is fired, covered again in the enamel and the piece is then re-fired until a reasonable thickness is achieved. Subsequently, colored enamels are added. In the re-firing process some contraction of the piece may take place when it cools producing a network of fine cracks throughout the bottle. Fashion meant that at times this was considered desirable and may sometimes be deliberately enhanced by the craftsman.

Cloisonné

Referred to as enamel filigree by the Chinese, but better known as *cloisonné*, this is generally regarded as an oriental art practiced mostly in China and Japan. Having developed since the Yuan dynasty and probably imported as part of the Arabic trade, *cloisonné* involves the laying of fine wires (generally copper) onto a metal body (also usually copper) to create a filigreed effect. The gaps between the wires or "*cloisons*", which are laid in a pattern, are filled with the enamel powder which incorporates semi-precious stones and is formed into a paste by mixing with water. Once the water has evaporated the whole piece is fired at very high temperature. This fuses the enamel powder together and also bonds it to the metal body and the *cloisons* creating a finished surface of one or two sixteenths of an inch thick.

Upon cooling, contraction of the enamel from the wires inevitably occurs leaving gaps that must be filled in by applying more enamel. The piece must then be re-fired. This process may be repeated several times. The fired item is then smoothed down and polished and edges of the wires left exposed are gilded. The post-firing item, be it snuff bottle or vase looks nothing like the finished product. It requires fairly aggressive polishing to remove the excess enamels and leave a level polished surface for which this type of enamel is famous. The end result is a beautiful object which is unlike any other in the art world.

The small nature of snuff bottles involving various small and oddly shaped *cloisons* of various colors makes it a demanding technique. As a result they were not ideally suited to this type of decoration and the number available either old or modern is small. Ones made with silver wire on either bronze or silver bodies are even less common and those with gold detailing are generally confined to museums.

The first recorded bottle of this kind appeared in the third year of the Emperor Qianlong's reign. As it appears in the *Zaobanchu* records it was clearly made in the Imperial workshops. Instead of being satisfied with a contrasting stopper in another material the Emperor ordered that a matching onc bc producccd, which must have been a very demanding task. Further records indicate the popularity of this material but also confirm the small numbers made. In the forty-third year of the same reign the eunuch *Hu Shejie* gave the workshops a pearl which was to be incorporated into the stopper of a round-waisted bottle.

Workshops both inside and outside the Palace produced bottles of this kind throughout the Qing period and yet they remain rare. Larger pieces such as bowls and vases are much more readily available confirming the difficulty of working on such a small scale.

Fine painted enamel on a copper bottle in the "Canton" style. A crane raises its head to the setting sun amid a landscape of lake and mountains. *Courtesy of Penny Collection*. £30-40. $40-55

Painted Enamelwork

Much more suitable to the purpose is enamel painting on metal. The technique for this type of work was imported from Europe during the reign of the Emperor Kangxi. He had almost certainly seen examples on gifts from envoys or foreign traders and wished to have it included in his own workshops. As with *cloisonné* the majority of bottles are on copper bodies though gold, silver and bronze examples are known.

After the application of a light colored enamel to the body of the bottle it is decorated with enamel paints, using a fine brush, and then fired to fuse the enamels together and to the bottle's surface. To avoid color running during firing the decoration tends to incorporate mainly fine lines and small dot type applications. The result is a very attractive and delicate object.

This type of work is generally referred to as Canton enamel because a high percentage of the enameling was done in Canton (Guangzhou). The majority of the pieces in the Imperial collection, however, were crafted in the Forbidden City's own workshops set up on the Emperor's instructions. Most of this was either by or under the supervision of a French enameller named *Gravereau* who arrived in Beijing in 1717 at the invitation of the Emperor Kangxi. Regrettably few detailed records remain from this period, having either been destroyed by one of the many fires suffered in the Forbidden City or removed to cover up the disappearance of articles at the end of the dynasty. There are, however, just ten bottles, each bearing the appropriate reign mark, which date from this time. These cannot be specifically credited to *Gravereau* because, like his Chinese colleagues, he was not permitted to sign his work.

The peak for painted enamel bottles came in the Yongzhen reign because he had a particular passion for them. In fact immediately upon ascending to the throne he ordered that the best enamellers in Guangzhou be brought to Beijing to join his own workshops. To increase output he established another workshop directly under his own control which lasted late into the Qianlong period. To ensure perfection the bottles ordered specifically were submitted for approval at each stage of production using drawings and wooden models even before the real work began.

Having a fondness for black, Yongzhen broke away from the usual style of a light background and ordered bottles with light colored blossom on a black background. This use of a darker ground was then extended to red upon which plum blossom was painted. Despite the Imperial taste for them, dark background bottles did not find general favor and so are very few in number.

Probably as a result of growing numbers of tributes and gifts, Emperor Qianlong developed a particular interest in things European. Unable to travel there himself he ordered numerous enameled objects, including snuff bottles, to be decorated with appropriate subjects such as elegant ladies and landscapes. These tend to look rather incongruous since the artists who painted them had only seen Europe in pictures. Nevertheless, the Imperial taste was satisfied and the fashion for this style grew.

Despite an apparent demand, the lack of good artists and the time necessary for each piece meant that production remained small. A record of seventy bottles produced in one year is deemed to have been high and needless to say examples of such works changing hands today are very rare indeed.

Imperial production of this type of bottle ended with the orders of Emperor Jiaqing in 1796 but continued in Guangzhou throughout the remainder of the dynasty. The historians of the Forbidden City Collection estimate that some 6,000 enamel painted bottles were produced in the hundred years or so of production prior to that date. How many of those are accounted for is not known as there is no overall data relating to the whereabouts of bottles in museum and private collections.

Bottles are still produced in Guangzhou workshops today by craftsmen using skills which have changed little over the years and have

A painted enamel on copper bottle in "Canton" style with fine brush work depicting a teacher with his young pupil in the mountains on one side. Another teacher with his assistant features on the opposite side. *Courtesy of Klemer Collection.* £60-80. $85-115

A "Canton" style painted enamel bottle on copper with portrait of a European lady with ringlets and a landscape. The black and yellow decoration which surrounds these two panels is unusual. *Courtesy of Klemer Collection.* £60-80. $85-115

been passed down through the generations. Painted enameling returned to Beijing in the mid-nineteenth century replicating, though not equaling, the styles of the earlier heyday periods. These later copies are often mistaken for their earlier counterparts especially as many bear "tribute" reign marks which suggest earlier origins. Differences in quality may be detectable to a real expert but undoubtedly many have been misidentified and with such high prices involved for these articles there is little wonder.

Champleve Enamels

The third category of enamels are best referred to as *champleve* since there seems to be no Chinese name by which they can be differentiated. In snuff bottle terms these are a very minor group which are usually confused with the two groups already mentioned. This type varies from the others in that the enamel colors are not separated by wires and are rarely painted, though in the West painted enamels, which are clearly not oriental, are usually categorized as *champleve*. Generally the enamels are more translucent than *cloisonné* and are applied in single or limited colors over a metal body which has been engraved or molded with a pattern. The enamels therefore highlight the engraved pattern by appearing to have different shades where the color is thicker. In a limited number of instances the enamels are also additionally decorated with enamel painting.

Three similar gourd shaped copper bottles with hand-painted enamel decorations. Even what might be described as "tourist" quality bottles such as these require considerable skill and work. £25-30 each. $35-40

A Qianlong reign mark shows the original inspiration behind this superbly painted enamel on copper bottle. An assistant is placing an inspirational stem of flowers into a narrow-necked bud vase for his master while on the opposite side, another pupil appears to be looking for a suitable gift. £120-150. $175-215

A fine and rare enamel snuff bottle. Mark and period of Qianlong (1736-1795), 49 mm. (A) £17,200. $24,600

Enamel on Glass

The firing temperature for enamels is close to the melting point of the glass, so a great deal of experimentation went on to add ingredients which would raise it above the critical level. There was some success and as a result a lovely range of enameled glass bottles emerged.

Most are decorated with elaborate tracery patterns, on opaque glass, which enabled the colors to remain separate instead of blending, as they tend to, under the heat. Others have been carved before the enameling so that the added color highlights the detail of the carving.

These bottles were the result of collaboration between the workshops set up for glass work and those for enameling, as the skills are so very different. An indication of the difficulty involved in this production process is the fact that only around three hundred such bottles were produced during the whole of the Yongzhen and Qianlong reigns. The Emperors themselves seem to have recognized the level of difficulty and only commissioned very small numbers. They did, however, regularly reprimand their craftsmen when failures occurred.

The rarity and delicacy of these bottles made them highly prized by the Emperors who had special boxes made for them and stored them in the treasury rather than having them on regular display. Unlike most other types of bottle, there are also few records of them having been granted as gifts to ministers or other dignitaries.

A carved and delicately enameled milk glass bottle with highlighted floral panels and Greek key pattern around the neck. £100-120. $145-175

A milk glass bottle with slight relief carving to enhance the detail of a basket of fruit and flowers. Both the basket and its contents of peach, pomegranate, blossoming branches, and chrysanthemum are enameled in *famille rose* colors. £60-80. $85-115

An opaque white glass bottle carved in the form of a ribbed melon with fine painted enamel tracery in *famille rose* colors. £80-100. $115-145

A miniature milk glass bottle carved and enameled with a cricket. *Courtesy of Penny Collection*. £50-60. $70-85

A clear slightly pink tinted bottle is here decorated with spring blossom and other flowers in well applied enamels. £50-60. $70-85

A milk glass bottle has been overlaid with green and polished back smoothly until the green outer layer is extremely thin except at the foot. The whole has then been enameled with angry looking dragons in a continuous pattern. £80-100. $115-145

Right and far right:
A very skilled hand has applied this pale blue enamel landscape to an opaque white glass bottle. The detail stands examination even under a magnifying glass. It highlights the qualities of some of the simpler pieces which make up a collection. £100-120. $145-175

Angular faceting is an unusual feature of this dark cobalt blue (appearing black) double gourd shaped bottle. Some panels are enameled in *famille rose* colors with dragonflies and butterflies. *Courtesy of Penny Collection*. £100-120. $145-175

Dark green glass (appearing black) has been outlined with an image of two ladies relaxing in pale green/gold enamel. On one side a woman holds a fan and a *mao bi* (writing brush) behind her back. The large characters "*shi nu tu*" translates simply as "beautiful lady picture". On the opposite side the large characters "*shi nu si qing*" translates as "beautiful lady thinking of her lover", suggesting that on the first side she was writing to him. The smaller characters are the same on both sides reading "*wu yin nian zuo*". The sixty year lunar calendar goes through the same set of year names every time making it rather difficult sometimes to precisely date an article even though it has been theoretically dated. The style and wear of this bottle lead us to conclude that the appropriate year is 1938, during the *Min Guo* period. £150-180. $215-260

A finely painted monochrome image in enamels of two women with bound feet sitting with a child. On the opposite side are three women with bound feet sitting together. £60-80. $85-115

Typical Chinese street workers are depicted on both sides of this milk glass bottle. The monochrome images show a barber with his stool and basin suspended on a pole across his shoulder and a street chiropodist attending to his client's foot. £60-80. $85-115

A fine enamel glass snuff bottle. Early twentieth century, 46 mm. (A) £1,400-1,750. $2,005-2,505

A rare and fine enamel glass snuff bottle. Early twentieth century, 63 mm. (A) £6,400-8,000. $9,155-11,440

Delicate enamel painting decorates this unusual small turquoise glass bottle which probably dates from the nineteenth century. £80-100. $115-145

A rare ruby glass snuff bottle. Mark and period of Qianlong (1736-1795), 69 mm. (A) £7,650. $10,940

A large opaque white glass bottle carved in relief with eight horses. The relief areas have then been enameled in a cartoon-like manner to depict the famous Eight Tang Horses, 4.0" (10 cm). £100-120. $145-175

A deep yellow bottle has been molded and carved in the stylized form of an elephant. The enamel decoration significantly enhances the relief shape. *Courtesy of Penny Collection*. £100-120. $145-175

Enamel on Porcelain

A group of porcelain bottles was also enameled rather than painted with the usual under-glaze colors. In some instances the enamel forms the glaze itself while in others the enamels are applied after the initial glazing process has been completed. While not strictly porcelain some of the best "*yi xing*" (terracotta) bottles are decorated in the first of those two ways. When the enamel has been applied in small dots or gem shaped designs this is usually referred to as beading or jewelling.

Modern research into the subject suggests that a large number of the enameled porcelain and glass bottles previously attributed to the Imperial workshops may have been created in the independent workshops of Beijing instead. Though bearing reign marks, their work is considered to have been slightly inferior to their regal colleagues.

Substantial relief carving gives the base for the delicate enameled painting on this milk glass bottle which shows pomegranate, peaches, finger citron and Chinese cabbage. £60-80. $85-115

A superbly carved cinnabar lacquer on copper bottle with its original stopper. One of China's minority ethnic groups is featured on one side in the form of a mother and child. £200-250. $285-360

Chapter Seven: Additional Materials

A definitive list of other materials used for snuff bottles is not a viable proposition since no catalogue exists of all of the bottles produced, either historically or more recently. The range known is enormous and it is always possible to create sub-categories in order to satisfy some collectors' desire for accuracy. However covering every possible variation would be almost impossible because someone would always have an extra obscure one to add.

In the following pages we have set out as many examples as possible without extending into the realms of obscurity. They will certainly cover the majority of types which the average collector is likely to encounter in the marketplace and probably some which he or she won't. The selection includes natural bottles made from fruit stones, bamboo, wood, gourds and coral as well as those in bronze, silver, bone, horn and lacquer.

Where possible, in this chapter, we have included as much detail as possible with each example so that the reader can see and understand without having to flick from page to page. Though the numbers are not large it is hardly surprising that many of the bottles in these categories were very popular among the Qing Court and remain so with modern collectors. The materials and their novel usage are among the most tactile and interesting of all and yet quite early examples are not generally expensive. This is probably because many traditional collectors do not consider them to be important or spectacular enough to fight over at auction.

Lacquer

Lacquer is the sap from the tree *Rhus vernicifera* found in China. The collected sap is clarified and colored by the addition of powdered minerals, most notably cinnabar, otherwise known as mercuric sulphide to produce a deep red color. The Chinese have been using lacquer since at least the Han period, a long time before snuff bottles came into existence, and its popularity flourished during the Yuan, Ming and Qing dynasties.

Snuff bottles with lacquer work are superb examples to illustrate the time and skill required to produce such bottles. The body of the snuff bottle is usually made of copper but may also be wood, brass or some other metal. Over this successive layers of cinnabar lacquer

Two European style people are featured on the flat panels of this cinnabar lacquer bottle which is superbly carved and is on a copper body. £180-220. $260-315

(often over two hundred layers, each layer being only the thickness of a thin coat of paint) are applied. Each layer must be allowed to dry before the next application can be made, so the production of cinnabar lacquer snuff bottles is a very time consuming and labor intensive process. Once the layering is complete the design is carved in relief style though there is no color contrast such as is found with the cameo glass carving. In the case of lacquer, which is a softer material, the expression "carving" is more apt since it is a selection of sharp hand tools which are used for the work. There is little margin for error in this work since it is impossible to replace small pieces removed by accident from this fragile material.

Small numbers of this type of bottle appear to have been produced throughout the Qing dynasty with popular designs including continuous landscapes, displays of flowers and complex legendary scenes. The hand of a master carver is always evident in the quality of the work.

Many bottles purporting to be made of cinnabar lacquer are in fact plastic or resin but the quality of carving and the tactile difference in the genuine lacquered bottles will usually distinguish them from the synthetic ones. Though the weight and texture may be similar to lacquer, most fakes have been molded as well as having a carved finish and almost invariably show signs of air bubbles, which do not occur in the genuine article.

A carved cinnabar lacquer snuff bottle. Middle Qing dynasty, eighteenth century, 62 mm. (A) £480-640. $690-915

Earthenware

Pottery (otherwise known as earthenware) snuff bottles are derived from clay and are fired at much lower temperatures (800-1100 degrees centigrade) than porcelain bottles. They are not impermeable and must be glazed if they are to contain any liquid. This material, very popular with traditional teapot collectors, is frequently referred to as *Yi Xing* and may be decorated with applied or painted enamels or clay slip in one or more contrasting colors. Originating from the town of *Yi Xing* just west of Shanghai this colored clay has been categorized as porcelain in some instances but its natural red clay color and unglazed appearance places it firmly as pottery for most collectors.

This and other simpler styles of bottle became popular in the nineteenth century among the literary classes who were not interested in the ostentation of the elaborate bottles but nevertheless wanted to follow the snuff fashion.

Cast in bronze, this bottle has the outward appearance of being carved cinnabar and may well have been molded from a bottle of that kind. The highly polished outer surface lends itself beautifully to this type of detail. Some of the inner detail will undoubtedly have been added after the casting. *Courtesy of Penny Collection*. £120-150. $175-215

Precious Metals

Both gold and silver bottles are rare since their base material would have been prohibitively expensive for all but the very wealthy. Many of those which were made for the Imperial Household would have disappeared in the chaos and poverty at the end of the Qing dynasty and were probably melted down to avoid identification. The very few examples which do exist are confined to museums and therefore cannot concern us greatly as potential collectors items. Other metals, such as copper, with a silvered finish do appear particularly in the form of filigree and overlay decoration for glass and stone bottles. The *cloisons* of a limited number of enameled bottles have also been made in silver.

A small delicate silvered bronze double gourd bottle mounted with a dragon on either side and a phoenix on the base. *Courtesy of Penny Collection*. £100-120. $145-175

A fine carved copper snuff bottle. Middle Qing dynasty, eighteenth century, 50 mm. (A) £11,500. $16,445

At first appearance this amber bottle is impressively carved as a monkey with two babies in her arms. Closer examination and experience reveal that it is in fact a reconstituted amber/resin mix. Amber being a natural resin anyway lends itself to this kind of reproduction. Such bottles are still not common and therefore have a place in the modern collector's market. *Courtesy of Penny Collection.* £25-35. $35-50

Amber

Amber is the fossilized resin of an extinct species of pine in the early Tertiary Period. It is often a transparent golden yellow or a rich brown in color though a whole range of other colors are encountered in jewelry. The Chinese regard amber as a symbol of longevity as they recognize and appreciate the time required in creating such a substance. Snuff bottles made of amber are warm to the touch, easily scratched and take a high polish. Amber snuff bottles also retain electricity. When amber is rubbed on woolen cloth, it will attract mustard seeds or other small objects. However, this is not a definitive test for genuine amber, as some plastics also retain electricity. Care must be taken with these bottles, as amber will absorb materials such as adhesives which can discolor it. When displaying amber snuff bottles, as with ivory, a small amount of atmospheric moisture should be provided. This can be done by placing a small cup of water in the cabinet with the snuff bottles. Amber should also be kept away from direct heat and sunlight as it is prone to splitting and cracking.

Another form, known as root amber, comes from the sap within the roots of the same extinct pine tree. Originating underground this unusual form of amber contains small amounts of soil giving it cloudy but interesting variations in color. The skilled craftsman in the design of a root amber snuff bottle may exploit these variations in color.

Some contemporary bottles are made, jigsaw like, from tens and even hundreds of small pieces of amber fragments polished and shaped to fit together to form bottles of various shapes. We have not been able to establish an historic precedent for this method but there may well be one. The result is fragile but very attractive.

Less desirable are snuff bottles composed of amberoid, the term used to describe a material composed of fragments of real amber which have been artificially reconstructed by means of heat, pressure or the mixing of the real amber resin with an artificial resin with similar properties and appearance. This material is usually molded but may have a carved finish.

Above and right:
This amber frog has been created like a three-dimensional jigsaw puzzle from dozens of small blocks of real amber. Constructed into a block, it has then been carved into the shape of a frog with the nose detaching to form the stopper. *Courtesy of Penny Collection*. £60-80. $85-115

Above and right:
A fantailed goldfish is a popular subject in any material and is here seen carved in lovely detail from a single piece of natural amber. The original stopper appears as a small jet of water spewing from the fish's mouth. £120-150. $175-215

A small round ivory bottle with four flattened panels to the main body and an ornately ringed neck. Middle Eastern in style, this may well have been made for a merchant plying the silk route, 1.25" (3.0 cm). *Courtesy of Klemer Collection*. £200-250. $285-360

A finely carved ivory double fish pair of bottles attached like Siamese twins. *Courtesy of Penny Collection*. £200-250. $285-360

Ivory

As one of the most highly regarded materials from which to make snuff bottles it is here that we find some of the most beautiful and some of the most expensive. The Chinese also regard ivory as having medicinal properties and as such ivory snuff bottles are seen as charms or talismans to ward off illness. Ivory carving workshops were among those established in the Forbidden City, though not exclusively for the production of snuff bottles. Emperor Yongzhen increased the number of fine craftsmen in the ivory workshop by importing selected workers from around China. It would appear that few bottles were directly ordered except when he saw examples in other materials which he then wished to have copied. Otherwise it was left to the carvers' imagination to produce original works to present to the Emperor at the times of the three main festivals.

As the ivory carvers were so skilled in their material, and also used to working on other subjects, most of the Imperial bottles are in the form of animals, birds and fruit hollowed in the normal way to produce a bottle. Few seem to be in the more standard snuff bottle forms of a rounded or square edged bottle but those which are tend to be engraved with a pattern or poetic calligraphy. To enhance this slight decoration colored inks may be rubbed into the engraved areas as a highlight. Unfortunately, as with other aspects of art during this period, the artists were not encouraged or permitted to sign their work. While extensive lists of names appear on record for the workshops there is little or no indication as to which artist produced which pieces. Not until the wind-down of the workshops during the Jiaqing reign did some of the craftsmen move to private workshops where they began to establish an identity.

Extensive world trading bans on ivory have made it very difficult to collect this type of bottle but a small number are available, as will be seen in the following pages. Many of the old ivory carvers, however, have turned their attentions to less contentious materials with the result that many new bone, nut and wood carvings are better than they would have been twenty years ago.

This unusual composite ivory bottle is probably Japanese in origin. It has been made with two thin layers of horn sandwiched between three layers of ivory which have then been hollowed, carved, and engraved. The detail of the two ladies has been rubbed with ink for emphasis. *Courtesy of Klemer Collection*. £250-300. $360-430

A superbly carved old ivory bottle with deep relief depicting a scholar and his servant beside a lake and beneath the trees, and the same scholar resting on the back of an ox and followed by his servant carrying a cash shaped basket on a pole. £1,800-£2,000. $2,575-2,860

An exquisitely carved and realistic cicada rests upon a leaf to form this lovely ivory bottle. The lack of ring holes shows that it was not intended for carrying as a pendant or belt accessory. £200-250. $285-360

An outstanding ivory bottle carved with fine detail depicting a Buddha-like figure sitting upon a lotus leaf-shaped cloud and holding a flaming pearl before a five-toed Imperial dragon. The whole scene is suspended above engraved waves. The same image appears on both sides. £1,800-2,000. $2,575-2,860

A pair of mandarin ducks on a lotus pond are balanced with the character "double happiness" on what is clearly a bottle intended for a marriage or anniversary. This old ivory piece would be a sought after object in the Far East where it would command a high price. *Courtesy of Klemer Collection*. £400-500. $575-715

A bulbous ivory bottle plugged at the top and bottom with additional ivory pieces. The extensive poem engraved and inked in fine detail dates from the Song dynasty and tells that in the north of China it is very cold and dry with a north wind and that when the snow falls, the trees look like blossoming pear. An old style lunar calendar date of "*wu chen nian xia yue*" tells us that this bottle was created in summer 1988. £400-500. $575-715

Unlike most similar bottles this Japanese ivory is carved from a single piece. The engraved detail to the side panels, foot, neck, and stopper have been highlighted with red and black lacquer. This is a very rare bottle and could command a high price in an international auction. *Courtesy of Klemer Collection*. £1,200-1,500. $1,720-2,145

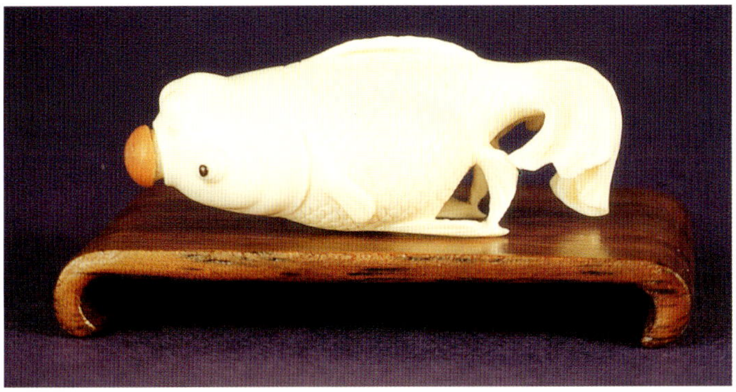

Above and right:
Fine detail on the fish scales and fins of this delicate little bottle set it apart from many of its contemporaries. The carver of this ivory miniature has taken considerable trouble with its design and detail. It is a pity that he has not signed his work. *Courtesy of Klemer Collection*. £200-250. $285-360

A deeply carved single sided bottle with a domestic scene viewed through an ornate window. *Courtesy of Aisingioro Collection. Photo by Ma Jun*. £800-900. $1,144-1,287

A pair of lovely double gourd shaped ivory bottles with finely engraved scenery and characters by artist *Chen Ji Pin*. These are some of his works from many years ago but at the age of eighty, he still carved and decorated one bottle per year and commands prices in excess of a thousand pounds for each. *Courtesy of Aisingioro Collection. Photo by MAaJun*. £2,000-2,500 for the pair. $2,860-3,575

A superb engraved ivory bottle by artist *Chen Ji Pin* with a landscape and extensive miniature calligraphy based upon a famous Song dynasty poem by *Ouyang Xiu* (1007-1072) called *Zui Weng Ting Ji* about the "Drunken Mens' Pavilion". The men in question are not intoxicated by wine but by the beauty of the mountain view which they see from the pavilion. The bottle tells us that engraver *Chen* was seventy-three years old when he created the bottle and a date of 1939 appears correct based upon the Chinese lunar calendar. The use of monkeys on the reverse of the bottle are a reference to someone being both intelligent and beautiful. It is therefore reasonable to assume that it was either commissioned as a special gift or designed with that intention. *Courtesy of Aisingioro Collection*. £1,500-1,700. $2,145-2,435

A finely carved ivory fish tangled among lotus stems and leaves. A small spurt of water forms the stopper. *Courtesy of Aisingioro Collection. Photo by Ma Jun*. £600-650. $860-930

The extensive miniature engraved calligraphy on this ivory bottle is of a quality rarely seen. Artist *Chen Ji Pin* tells us that he was seventy-two years old when this bottle was completed and makes reference to a particular day in the Chinese calendar which is the ninth of September (1938). The number "nine" means "*yang*" and on this day was therefore "double *yang*" which together with the sun and the moon refers to the harvest time of a person's life. It is therefore a celebration of a long life (presumably his own) on what is often referred to in China as "Old People's Day".

The main text is based upon a poem almost one thousand years old by *Ouyang Xiu* (1007-1072) and refers to what is known as the "Drunken Mens' Pavilion" where the visitors are not intoxicated by wine but by the beauty of the view in the surrounding mountains. The scene is therefore engraver *Chen*'s interpretation of the poem with men heading towards the pavilion over land and water. *Courtesy of Aisingioro Collection*. £1,500-1,700. $2,145-2,435

Bone has long been a poor man's substitute for ivory and should not be considered as any form of faking. This lovely example of a bone snuff bottle has excellent carving depicting a lady on a balcony and has buffalo horn at the foot and collar. £30-40. $40-55

Tortoise Shell

Tortoise shell is obtained from the Hawk's bill turtle found in the Malay Archipelago and Indian Ocean. The material is very fragile and is usually fabricated in sections. Small numbers of snuff bottles exist usually with the shell overlaid on fine wooden carcasses. As the shell is so thin and fragile little additional embellishment is usually found other than fine engraving.

Other animal products used for snuff bottles include rhinoceros horn, deer antler, buffalo horn, bone and whales teeth, though the list is probably endless. Each of these are in small numbers and some are the subjects of modern export and import bans so few are likely to be encountered.

This lovely tortoise shell bottle appears to have an interesting history. Its apparent provenance would make it very desirable but is difficult to prove. The four characters on one side read "*hong shu tang chang*" translating as "wild swan book room keep". Typically artists and writers gave poetic names to their favorite rooms and buildings so this may be a reference to either but does suggests a library. On the opposite side the five characters read "*Tan Zi Tong zheng yong*". "*Zheng yong*" is a request for the owner to carefully use and keep (presumably the bottle) and *Tan Zi Tong* is the name of a late Qing revolutionary writer who lived from 1865 to 1898. Having studied in the west, he returned to China and wanted it to modernize but was later executed as a revolutionary. The characters engraved into the tortoise shell have been highlighted with rubbed gold suggesting that it was an important possession rather than an attempt at a modern copy. He would also not have been an obvious choice for the faker because he is little known outside China. £300-500. $430-715

Wood

This is an interesting category since there are two groups of bottles which fall into it. It is also one which is overlooked by many collectors who regard wood as an inferior material despite the fact that these bottles can be beautifully worked and even the old ones are affordable. The first group are the bottles made specifically to be used for containing snuff, which became popular, like the *Yi Xing* bottles, in the later Qing years. Their simplicity was an attraction to the growing intellectual class. The second group, which are difficult to identify, are those bottles which started life as prototypes given to the Emperor before work on some of the more expensive bottles began. Only if one had the prototype and the end product together or the prototype and some accompanying drawings could one be sure. It is interesting to speculate then, with this group, whether the Emperor himself may have handled any particular example.

The age of wooden bottles rarely comes into question because it is very difficult to achieve the patination or signs of age artificially without them being obvious. Surprisingly, in the circumstances, wooden bottles remain inexpensive, perhaps being beneath the standard of some collectors.

A carved wooden frog rests on a lotus leaf with a bud acting as stopper and a lotus pod the foot. Lovely detail makes this a desirable item. £120-150. $175-215

An unusual wooden bodied bottle with applied chagrin (shark skin). £80-100. $115-145

A beautifully simple turned hardwood vase shaped bottle with slight burr detail. Style and wear indicate that this is nineteenth century or earlier. *Courtesy of Penny Collection*. £150-200. $215-285

An oblong wooden bottle with two inset engraved bone panels showing an elegant lady beside a stream and a young girl dreaming as she looks into the distance. *Courtesy of Penny Collection*. £100-120. $145-175

Deeply carved boxwood bottle. £50-60. $70-85

Deeply carved and pierced boxwood bottle with a tall neck depicting a domestic scene in a mountain home. £50-60. $70-85

Right and below:
A small bamboo bottle which was probably used to sell a commercial brand of snuff to be used either directly or decanted into a more ornate version. In archaic form the characters read "*qi sang*" translating as "strange/different enjoy". This brand name or variety name is enhanced on the opposite side by an engraving of winter plum blossom which in itself symbolizes life through winter or adversity. Nineteenth century. £40-50. $55-70

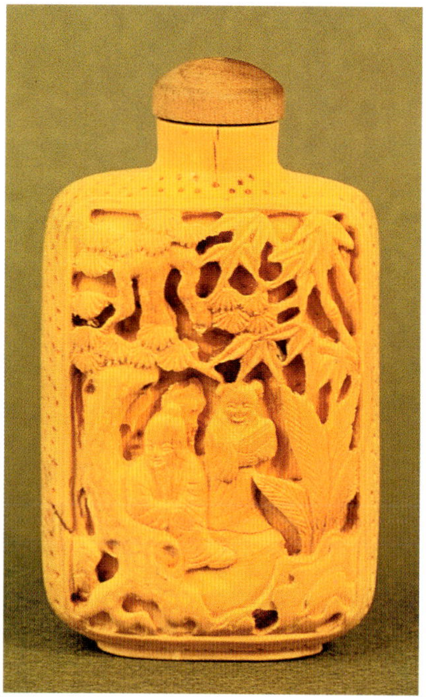

A square-shouldered boxwood bottle with deep relief carving to both sides. £50-60. $70-85

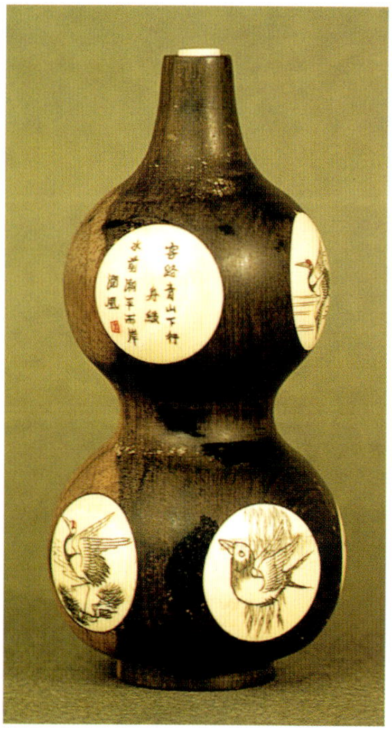

A carved rosewood bottle in the form of a double gourd inset with circular ivory panels. The lower panels are decorated with engraved birds and the upper ones contain poetic texts about a crane and other birds flying through the area to enjoy the beautiful views and gentle breeze in the green mountains. The signature is illegible. £100-120. $145-175

A boxwood snuff bottle. Middle Qing dynasty, eighteenth century, 100 mm. (A) £2,400-3,300. $3,435-4,720

A pale boxwood bottle delightfully carved as a fish among lotus stems and leaves with multi-layered piercing. £100-120. $145-175

Right and below:
This intricately carved boxwood fish is at the better end of this type of bottle. Some boxwood pieces are so crude as to be not worth bothering with but the attention to detail in this instance has resulted in a worthwhile object. *Courtesy of Penny Collection.* £80-100. $115-145

An elegant tall turned wooden bottle, rather reminiscent of a European bell pull. Late nineteenth century satin wood. £100-120. $145-175

Above and right:
A lovely double gourd shaped burr wood bottle which is extremely tactile. Probably nineteenth century because of the patination which has occurred through long handling. £150-200. $215-285

Above and right:
The history of this wooden bottle is not entirely certain. It is quite clearly old and probably over a hundred and fifty years old but what is uncertain is whether it was made for use in its own right or as a sample for a far more precious object. Many such pieces were initially carved in wood to obtain the Emperor's approval before the lapidary began work on a precious piece of jade or other material. The amount and quality of detail applied to such a simple object would definitely suggest a higher purpose. £150-200. $215-285

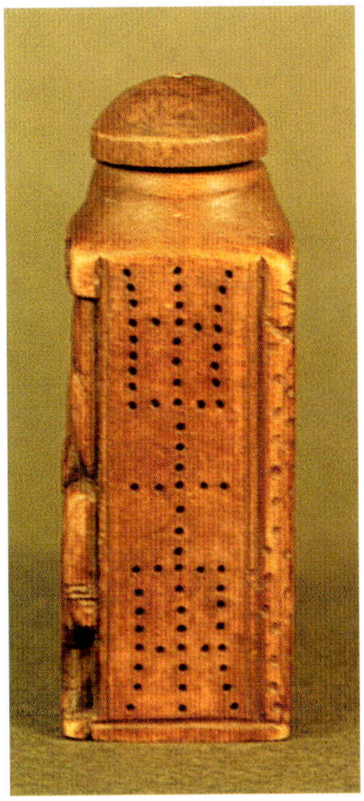

Left and above:
An unusually shaped wooden bottle deeply carved on each side with images of a boy trying to tame a dragon and beating off a fierce tiger. The flat end panel has the character "*shou*" ("long life") punched into it in tiny dots. £80-100. $115-145

Left and above:
A delightfully tactile old burr wood bottle which needed no embellishment. *Courtesy of Penny Collection*. £120-150. $175-215

A cylindrical carved bamboo bottle with turned wood base and top panels. The carving shows a young boy with a branch appearing to follow a hermit in a rocky landscape. £80-100. $115-145

An unusual bottle which was initially difficult to identify but was finally revealed as carved coconut inlaid with shell and malachite. This extraordinary combination would have been difficult to create, especially bearing in mind the shape of the bottle. It still defies logic but the material is undoubtedly coconut shell. *Courtesy of Penny Collection*. £80-100. $115-145

Nuts and Seeds

Much to many people's surprise this group formed an important part of the early snuff bottle group. It was perhaps the challenge to find new styles and materials to fulfill a voracious demand which prompted the craftsmen to look in this direction. Among those found here are a mango seed mounted in silver and a nut, resembling a brazil, mounted with a metal collar to protect it. Like the wooden ones these are generally inexpensive but make an interesting addition to a collection. Others known to exist include peach stones, orange peel and coconut shell. Part of this group but with a category of their own are the gourd bottles.

A pair of preserved red pine cones mounted with bone collars and stoppers are an extraordinary and imaginative choice for these snuff bottles. £300-400 the pair. $430-575

A silver mounted large preserved seed possibly from a mango. The use of silver at the foot, shoulders, and neck reduces the deterioration of the bottle's body. The characters on the coin read from right to left and top to bottom, "*fu zai yan qian*" translates literally as "good luck there eyes front", or more realistically "may good luck come soon." £120-150. $175-215

A baked nut with beautiful natural surface decoration has been hollowed and given a brass collar and screw stopper to create this unusual bottle. Decomposition means that few of these have survived and are sought after by serious collectors. Probably around eighty to a hundred years old. £100-120. $145-175

Below:
A small double gourd has been mounted with a silver collar to protect it from repeated use around the neck. A similar protection has been added in the form of a decorative silver foot though the bottle will not stand upright. £50-60. $70-85

Molded Gourds

Over 1,000 gourd snuff bottles are known to have been made during the Qing dynasty. A large number of these were grown in the private Imperial gardens where they could be watched over by their anxious growers.

The art of molding the gourds as they grow, to create specific shapes or relief decoration, was introduced from the countryside, probably during the Kangxi reign, and resulted in many objects including bowls, vases, dishes and, of course, snuff bottles. While this might appear to be a relatively simple partnership between man and nature in reality very few of the gourds each season were successful and suitable for the craftsmen to work with. Harvested in August or September they were given to the lacquer workshops for preserving and then passed on to others for finishing with either a metal or ivory collar to the neck. Needle scratching of a pattern to the outer finish of the gourd was a popular form of decoration, usually rubbed with colored ink for highlighting.

Left and above:
A finely molded gourd snuff bottle. Qing dynasty Daoguang (1821-1850), 64 mm. (A) £8,000-10,000. $11,440-14,300

A rare small gourd snuff bottle. Middle Qing dynasty, eighteenth century, 42 mm. (A) £7,650. $10,940

Coral

A small carved pink coral bottle with small white dots of natural imperfections. The character "*shou*" ("long life") and "*fu*" ("good luck") are carved in relief as the principle decoration. *Courtesy of Klemer Collection.* £200-250. $285-360

A lion's head and feet are carved in relief from part of this branch coral bottle which has been color enhanced. *Courtesy of Penny Collection.* £100-120. $145-175

A color enhanced branch coral bottle carved with a fearsome guardian mask. £100-120. $145-175

A roaring animal head is carved into this branch coral bottle. £100-120. $145-175

A carved coral snuff bottle. Qing dynasty, nineteenth century, 38 mm. (A)
Estimate £1,000-1,200. Achieved £3,060. $4,375

Horn

These two miniature horn bottles resemble chess pieces and clearly have a Persian influence in their design. Carved with fine detail, they probably originate from the far west of China or have been created by someone born in that region. *Courtesy of Penny Collection*. £100-120. $145-175

The horn body of this unusual bottle is partially encased in a filigreed and silvered copper jacket inset with small pieces of turquoise. The matching stopper is attached to the main bottle by a chain. One of the small number of similar bottles originating from Tibet, it is not exactly pretty but is a very interesting collector's item. £150-200. $215-285

Chapter Eight: Inside Painting

The technique of painting the inside of snuff bottles may have been invented by the artist *Gan Xuanwen* who, it is claimed, established the *Lingnan* School of inside-painted snuff bottles. This artist worked on bottles during the Jiaqing reign (1796-1820). This belief appears to be based upon two reign marked bottles for the fifteenth and twenty-first years of the Jiaqing reign. The historians of the Forbidden City, however, favor a much later date since no other bottles can be traced which are verifiable for another fifty years. As the Jiaqing reign was also at the height of snuff bottle popularity it is unlikely that such a wonderful innovation would have been allowed to disappear.

Since the serious development of this art form did not take place until the much later Guangxu reign it seems likely that the earlier development claims may be based upon bottles given earlier marks, a decoration technique common to many other types of bottles as well. For this and the other reasons stated we would have to concur with the later development belief.

Colorfully dressed beautiful ladies appear regularly in inside painted bottle art. Here they are seen in a set of three by the same artist who has used landscapes on the reverse of each. *Courtesy of Skippen Collection.* £60-80 each. $85-115

Early inside painted snuff bottles are often not as detailed and finely worked as more modern pieces and are thus perceived as cruder than contemporary versions. This may reflect the refinement of the technique over the years. A very good inside-painted snuff bottle is like a captured miniature painting or a piece of art on canvas with the older ones tending to have less elaborate painting on a more traditional decorative theme. It appears that the inside-painted bottle is like a blank canvas for the contemporary artist to expand and explore his or her skills in not only painting in miniature, but painting under near impossible constraints. It is, after all, a technique which requires the artist to paint in reverse and to do that through the narrow neck of a bottle. The shape of many bottles also suggests the near impossibility of decorating them on the inside as the artist is challenged to reach around corners to paint the inner shoulders.

As late arrivals on the snuff bottle scene, it was useful in many ways that the actual habit of snuffing was declining and that most collectors, including the Emperors, were exactly that, collectors. The delicacy of the inside painting and its general vulnerability meant that they were not really suitable for carrying snuff, though many were used for it, and that it was a modern style collectors' market which emerged. This is probably why many purist collectors of today ignore them because they are not seen as true useable snuff carriers. To do so, however, is to ignore a beautiful miniature art form.

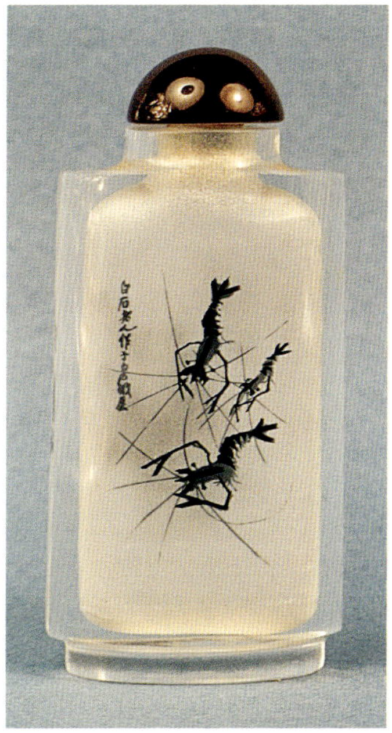

A beautifully simple squared glass crystal bottle decorated in black with prawns. *Courtesy of Skippen Collection*. £60-80. $85-115

A heavy rounded glass crystal bottle with images of tigers. *Courtesy of Skippen Collection*. £160-180. $230-260

Three typical monochrome decorated glass crystal bottles. *Courtesy of Skippen Collection*. £60-80 each. $85-115

A small blown glass bottle with monochrome painted historic street scene backed with gold leaf. *Courtesy of Klemer Collection*. £60-80. $85-115

With Imperial interest in snuff bottles having remained high for most of the previous two hundred years, and the quantity amassed in the Forbidden City running into tens of thousands, there is little wonder that this new idea captured the Emperor's attention.

The first examples recorded in the Forbidden City archives, in the reign of Emperor Guangxu (1875-1908), indicate that around thirty artists became famous for their work as the craft reached its height. Palace favorites were soon established resulting in several family dynasties of inside bottle painters being formed with techniques and styles being passed guardedly from father to son. Prominent among these early painters was the landscape artist *Zhou Leyuan* who was known for his bold style and ability to develop layers of paint as though they were on unrestricted paper.

One of the factors which reinforce the opinion that inside painted bottles found favor with the Royal Court is that they allowed themselves to be the subjects for portraits. Unlike their western counterparts, whose palaces and galleries are adorned with hundreds of family oil paintings, the Chinese Court was much less documented in a "photographic" sense. Many of the images which have been handed down as scroll paintings have been damaged or destroyed but a large number of them are also stylized, rather than being true representations of the individuals. Of course, by the time inside bottle portraits were being painted, photographs were a relatively common occurrence among the wealthy, even in China, and would probably have relieved the subjects from sitting for their portraits. They do, nevertheless, offer an excellent record of the prominent members of the Court and some of the high officials.

The ousting of the Emperor and the isolation of the Imperial Household in 1912 removed the demand and impetus for the creativity associated with them. This applied to all forms of craft for which the Court had been the main buyer and fashion setter, including snuff bottles. Fortunately, however, the art was passed down through the generations and was even revived by *Mao Zedong* so that several well-known painting families today claim a continuous heritage back to the nineteenth century.

In China the finest contemporary painters are highly regarded and as this is seen as a uniquely Chinese art form their work appears regularly among the treasured gifts to foreign dignitaries. There are many families whose work merits mention and several whose work appears in the following pages. High on the list is the *Xu* family whose painting founder is *Xu Pengqi*, originally from Hebei Province, a fine artist of varied style who has trained extensively in various painting techniques before devoting his time to inside bottle painting. Son *Xu Bu* and daughter *Xu Zhuojing* have also taken up the brush, following in their father's footsteps but developing styles of their own. Their regular customers include many collectors from around the world as well as the Chinese Foreign Ministry. Their works have also toured the world as ambassadors for China visiting some eighty-five countries. It is interesting to note that their permanent base in Beijing is in its famous antiques street Liulichang. Buyers of one of *Xu Pengqi's* better bottles, which can take six months to paint, can expect to pay around £5,000-£6,000 even

A tiny faceted glass crystal bottle featuring a simple but skillfully painted landscape, 1.0" (2.2 cm). *Courtesy of Klemer Collection.* £80-100. $115-145

An unusual bottle in blown glass with black detailing and a large single character for "*shui*" ("water") balanced by stylized image of water on the reverse. The character and the image are symbols rarely used in this type of decoration and it is unknown why it would have been painted but was probably commissioned for a particular purpose. £100-120. $145-175

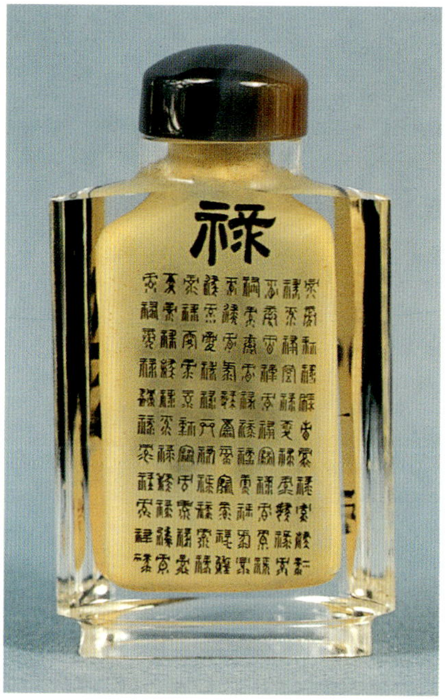
禄

寿
己卯春月作

禄
己卯春月作

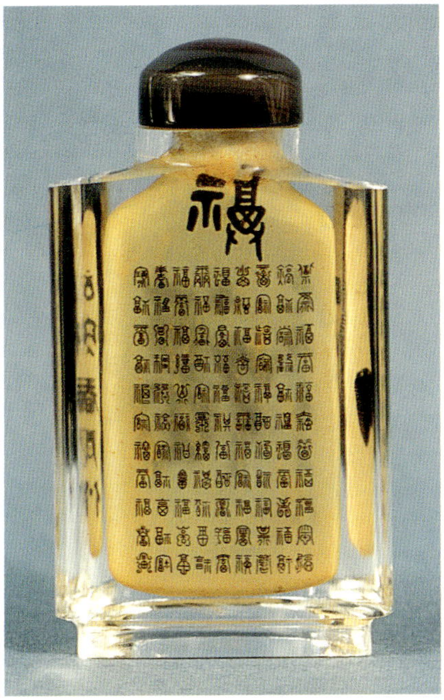

These four bottles have solely calligraphy decoration and are unusually shaped glass crystal. Each bottle represents only one word though it is repeated in one hundred different styles and ways including ancient forms of calligraphy and different words with the same meaning. This is a modern Chinese way to offer a hundred wishes of good luck. The calligraphy used in these bottles is of a very high standard and bears a single chop mark or signature with the name "*Lan*" which means "blue" but is most often used as a girl's name. The five character mark beside each of the large symbols reads "*yi mao chun yue zuo*" translating as "1999 spring month made" in the lunar calendar. *Courtesy of Skippen Collection*. £100-120 each. $145-175

direct from the artist but in doing so will join a very high ranking group of fellow owners which includes world leaders and royal households.

With little known about the development and initial reason for this beautiful but tortuous art form it has been suggested to us by some of the most devoted Chinese collectors that it must have been instigated by a Buddhist. This may not seem a particularly profound statement, since a high percentage of the Chinese followed this religion, but it does reflect the reverence shown to the artists for their extreme discipline and concentration which tends, even now, to be associated with Buddhist monks and aesthetes.

The essence of all snuff bottles is their small scale and the narrow neck through which the snuff passes on a small spoon. An individual who has not seen an inside-painted bottle and the degree of detail it contains could not comprehend the skill and patience involved. To the unskilled, passing a thin wire through the narrow hole traditional in snuff bottles is hard enough, let alone a paintbrush loaded with paint. Adding to the complication is the fact that the image must be constructed in reverse and allows no margin for error, since corrections are almost impossible to make. Some basic bottles may be designed so that the artist creates an outline, usually in black, and then fills in the spaces with colors. More complex and elaborate subjects such as portraits or subtle landscapes require much more in the way of layering of the color and a real understanding of what will happen as the picture is built up, in reverse, from the first brush stroke.

As we have said, there is no margin for error, because every brush stroke is visible from the outside of the bottle and cannot easily be painted out or erased. The other problem area is the mouth of the bottle which is susceptible to being caught with the loaded brush. Though a few small strokes may be considered acceptable at the mouth of a cheap bottle, an important artist's reputation would not permit him such an error of concentration so a work which had taken many weeks would have to be discarded or sold, unsigned, to a less discerning collector.

The principal market for modern bottles lies not, as suggested by other writers, with tourists but with increasingly wealthy Chinese and Taiwanese collectors. A limited number of serious westerners are beginning to realize the potential, as are a few museums, but many diehards remain to be convinced. In

The unusual shape of this bottle and its painted image make it an interesting collector's item. The glass crystal has been curved at the front and left flat at the back of the bottle. The principal image is one of another inside painted snuff bottle with a lion painted in it. The reverse of the bottle is a simple bamboo landscape. Signed. £100-120. $145-175

the meantime it leaves the way open for a new group of collectors to establish themselves. An increasing amount of information about some of the new artists and their work is already emerging and recently some of the top auction houses have included inside painted bottles, described as "Twentieth Century", in their oriental art sales. With no specific dates attributed to them they are likely to have been late examples rather than early ones but they were still estimated with high prices.

The end of Imperial China and the years which followed up to and after 1949 were not conducive to creativity of this or any other kind. The country was almost completely closed to the West and generally languished in poverty and suppressed opinion so there were few potential customers.

After 1949, however, with *Mao Zedong* at the helm, China looked towards many of its artisans and workers for inspiration. Many scholars were ridiculed and their ideas discredited but the artisans generally found favor. Strange then that, despite its connections with an Imperial past, the skill or art of inside bottle painting found a new sponsor with *Mao* himself setting up schools or academies for the redevelopment and expansion of the craft. Many of the older painters, whose work is revered today, owe their training and skill to this era, even though at the time most of their output was propagandist and featured characters from the revolution or their sayings. This particular group of bottles make an interesting collection though they are increasingly hard to find. *Mao* himself was the subject of numerous excellent portrait bottles as well as attempts to recreate his calligraphy style under the incredible restrictions of a bottle interior.

Watching an inside bottle painter at work, for any length of time, is a joy and an inspiration but will almost certainly give the observer a headache. Few of us are accustomed to the level of concentration necessary.

There are no limits to the decoration of snuff bottles generally other than those of the artist's skill and imagination. Although many contemporary artists have attempted to break away from the traditions of their training, very few have the skill such as the *Xu's* to carry it off. Some extend the ranges of their work into new original ideas while others emulate their western inspirers with incredible skill. The skill of the artists who painted famous frescoes throughout Europe is unquestioned, but how much more so that of the Chinese who have recreated them with such miniature and restricted accuracy. Little wonder, then, that some of these bottles are finding their way into important new collections.

A collector in England recently commented of a bottle painted "after" the style of a *Botticelli* masterpiece that the original was exquisite, the inside bottle painted one was "awesome". Not only had it been miniaturized with such skill it was done with unenviable restrictions which *Botticelli* himself would not have contemplated.

A blown amber glass bottle with simple but faded decoration shows the deterioration which can occur over time to inside painted bottles. This one almost certainly dates from the mid to late nineteenth century and still makes a good addition to any collection. £150-200. $215-285

Beautiful red blossom leaps vibrantly from the inside of this heavy glass crystal bottle hollowed with a double gourd shaped interior. £150-180. $215-260

In looking for this type of bottle it is worth noting that the majority of good ones will bear a small red signature or chop (seal) mark identifying the artist. Often a simplified or stylized character of the artist's name, they can be very difficult to read especially as some may be little more than a squiggle, rather like many western signatures. This usually indicates that the artist has graduated from one of the inside bottle painting academies or schools and is a painter of some note though the buyer should always assess whether the skill shown in the painting matches the price asked or, indeed, the presence of a signature.

Western and imitative works are rarely signed, the artists regarding it as an anomaly to have their chop mark on a portrait of President *Kennedy* or landscape of a New England Autumn. For most collectors this should be of little consequence, the quality of the painting speaking for itself, and the presence of most signatures being little more than a name anyway. Skilled collectors will begin to recognize their favorite artists purely by their style.

A bottle we sold in 1999 for £400 changed hands three times in four days rising to £1,600 by the time it was sold to an American museum scout who recognized the hand of the painter he was looking for even though there was no mark of any kind. Even without such knowledge it was an outstanding work of art worthy of the price it achieved.

As a final note on the subject it must be said that not all bottles are painted on the same material and this can be an important factor in determining a suitable price. A very small number of early and later bottles are made of natural rock crystal, agate or jade and have been polished to shape and then hollowed out to such an extent that the

Right:
A pretty blown glass bottle showing a landscape and a lady washing linen in a stream. Some characters but unsigned. *Courtesy of Skippen Collection*. £50-60. $70-85

bottle is almost transparent. They can then be painted on the inside in the same way as glass. Such bottles are highly prized and can be very expensive. Far more bottles are made of lead glass known in the West as crystal. These bottles are also created from a solid piece and are hollowed out, faceted and polished to the desired shape. They are generally quite heavy and the thick crystal glass of the sides creates effective magnifying and prismatic qualities which enhance the paintings. Such bottles tend to be better painted, as the initial materials are too expensive for the artists to produce shoddy work. The hollowing process used for both of the above types of bottles creates a fairly course inner surface which is ideally suited to the inks used for painting. It allows them to adhere to the "frosted" surface in the same way as it might to paper or canvas.

Most of the less expensive bottles, especially those referred to as tourist quality, are made of standard transparent glass blown into molds. These have little weight, can be cheaply bought by the painters and tend to have the amateur and student quality work within them. To create the desired surface for painting these bottles are treated to a wash of acid inside which slightly frosts the surface.

There has been a move in recent years to imitate inside painted bottles using a photographic method of transferring the color into the bottles but this has proved unsuccessful and would only fool the most naive of buyers. The color definition on these bottles is very poor, the inner surface is not evenly decorated and the overall appearance is shoddy. Collectors need have no fear that this method will improve since the equipment, investment and years of experimentation necessary would not be viable.

Two figures in red stand on rocky outcrops overlooking fast flowing mountain rivers and waterfalls. Beautifully painted inside glass crystal bottle, 4.5" (11 cm). £200-220. $285-315

Left:
A blown glass bottle with the animal images of a fox and a raccoon well painted in their natural habitat. £100-120. $145-175

Rats, cattle, dogs, and pigs, give animal appeal to these two unusual bottles. Each, of course, represents a Chinese year sign with two appearing per bottle. The complex characters in each explain the qualities and characteristics of those born in each represented year. The vivid colors contrast well with the white and black backgrounds. £160-180 each. $230-260

A heavy glass crystal bottle containing a modern landscape interpretation in an almost cubist style dominated by olive green. £150-180. $215-260

A glass crystal bottle depicting a group of men at the beginning of a mountain climb. £160-180. $230-260

Opposite page, top:
A large heavy glass crystal bottle hollowed with a double gourd shape and decorated predominantly with blue in a representation of a moonlit seascape with palm trees in the foreground and a moonlit landscape during snowfall. As representations of summer and winter this bottle may have been intended to be one of a pair showing the four seasons. The unusual coloring makes this a particularly striking example, 4.5" (11 cm). £180-200. $260-285

Opposite page, bottom:
The images of a rocky landscape in this heavy glass crystal bottle appear to be fragments of a larger picture rather than a continuous image. They are however, very effective and well painted, 4.5" (11 cm). *Courtesy of Skippen Collection*. £180-200. $260-285

This page:
Four wonderful images of Chinese opera masks decorate these two glass crystal bottles. £60-80 each. $85-115

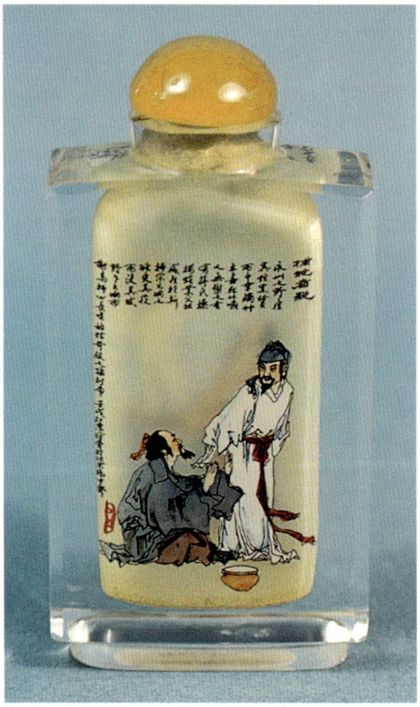

A glass crystal bottle painted with two men discussing philosophy which is set out above them in the calligraphy with a landscape on the reverse. £50-60. $70-85

An unspecified Emperor looks to one of the Eighteen Lohan for inspiration. On the reverse is a snow-covered lake landscape. £50-60. $70-85

A relatively few simple brush strokes with black ink create a surprisingly striking landscape against a yellow background in this blown glass bottle. *Courtesy of Skippen Collection*. £100-120. $145-175

Both the appearance and the calligraphy of these bottles confirm their age as early twentieth century. Both appear to have been used for storage of snuff which is unusual for inside painted bottles. The simple painting is highlighted with areas of white. Both bottles are blown glass and carry calligraphy dating them to what is known as the "*Min Guo*" period between the end of the Qing dynasty and the forming of the People's Republic in 1949. One refers to the seventh year (1918) and the other to the eighth year (1919). The images are based upon Buddhist temple subjects and have a propaganda nature. Without any specific text they represent the expression that "to learn, it is better to go ten thousand miles than to read ten thousand books". £200-250 each. $285-360

A praying mantis makes an unusual subject on both sides of this simple but attractive bottle. £80-100. $115-145

A rounded glass crystal bottle probably intended as a wedding gift shows two pairs of birds in the spring and winter seasons, symbolically wishing fidelity and a long life together. £120-140. $175-200

An unusual combination of cameo glass and inside painting has given us this attractive old bottle, probably from the nineteenth century, which appears to have been used to contain snuff. The clear and amethyst glass allow a single panel on each side upon which a simple image has been painted with the faces of the subjects highlighted in white. *Courtesy of Skippen Collection*. £100-150. $145-215

An excellent blown glass portrait bottle of *Mao Zedong* intended for propaganda purposes. *Mao* wrote a lot of poems and this is one of them reproduced in the style of his own handwriting. The subject is the *Lu Shan* mountains where he spent many summers and he writes that "the most beautiful places are the most dangerous to get to". The literal translation is quite pretty but the veiled meaning is that "having reached the top it is a dangerous place". Although not dated this bottle was almost certainly painted during the Cultural Revolution or his later years of political turmoil. As such it is a rare and very collectible object. £200-250. $285-360

The Chinese have regularly sort intellectual inspiration in the mountainous landscapes of the south of the country. Both sides of this decorative glass crystal bottle depict such scenes. *Courtesy of Skippen Collection*. £180-200. $260-285

A rounded glass crystal bottle which shows three bullock carts being pulled across a rather unsatisfactory bridge in a snow-covered landscape and the later progress of one of them through the countryside. £160-180. $230-260

A large glass crystal bottle depicting "*zhui ba xian*" ("eight drunken Immortals"). Further characters "*xin yi san yue hua*" tell us that painter "*Hua*" created this in March 2001 in the Chinese sixty year lunar calendar, 4.5" (11 cm). £200-250. $285-360

The famous Chinese story of Monkey is seen here in this wonderful painting. Fed up with living in Heaven, Monkey one day smashed everything around him and left because he wanted to be like a human. Stories of his subsequent exploits are endless and probably form the inspiration for many other bottles. The calligraphy beside the painting reads "*da nao tian gong*" which if translated literally means "big naughty sky palace trouble". Further characters "*xin yi nian zuo*" equate to "2001 year painted", 4.5" (11 cm). £200-250. $285-360

Richly painted historic street scenes embellish the two levels of this glass crystal bottle with a double gourd shaped hollowed interior. Incredible detail is the main feature of this bottle, 4.5" (11 cm). *Courtesy of Skippen Collection*. £200-250. $285-360

Both sides of this large double gourd interior glass crystal bottle show a freely painted image in monochrome of prawns. The simplicity and free hand in this decoration are the key, 4.5" (11 cm). *Courtesy of Skippen Collection*. £180-200. $260-285

A large lump of glass crystal has been hollowed into this double snuff bottle and vibrantly painted with images of the four seasons.

A large hollowed glass crystal bottle beautifully painted with brightly colored dragons, 4.5" (11 cm). £180-200. $260-285

A uniquely Chinese mountain landscape depicted in vibrant colors is the key to this artist's success. *Courtesy of Skippen Collection*. £200-250. $285-360

One of the hardest things to achieve in this medium is reflections upon water. Probably as a challenge this artist has chosen to have still water on one side and rough water on the other of this superb bottle. The subtlety of color would be enviable in any form of painting but is astounding when seen in this format. *Courtesy of Skippen Collection*. £250-300. $360-430

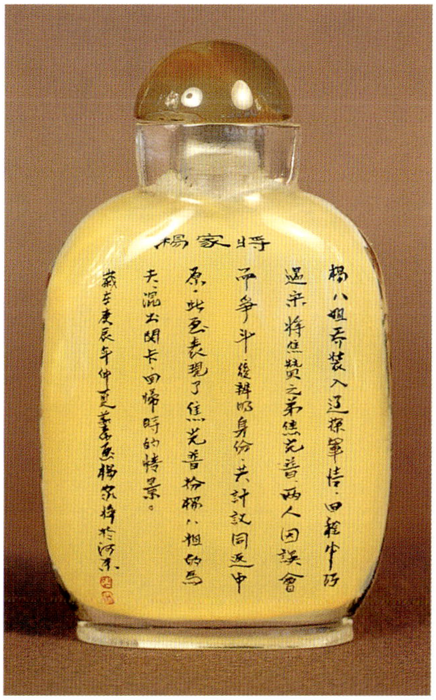

This superb glass crystal bottle depicts the famous story of the *Yang* family. Three successive generations worked for the Emperor (it is not known which), the grandmother being of royal line. Her three sons died for the Emperor as did her grandson. Her eight granddaughters also became warriors. The youngest *Yang Ba Jie* dressed as the enemy to infiltrate their lines. The other character *Jiao Guang Pu* also dressed as the enemy for the same purpose. When the two met they began to fight until they realized they were on the same side. The indistinct signature on this bottle appears to give us the name *Ge Yan*. £400-500. $575-715

A European cathedral style image of the Madonna and Child is beautifully painted in this rounded glass crystal bottle. The artist's impression of an unknown cathedral appears on the reverse. Such bottles are extremely difficult to paint well and are becoming very sought after. £400-500. $575-715

A large glass crystal bottle with very detailed landscape including mountains, buildings, and lakes. £220-250. $315-360

Both the coloring and the shape of this glass crystal bottle are unusual. The vultures depicted are also uncommon subjects for Chinese art. £200-250. $285-360

Peacocks and other birds are painted superbly in this glass crystal bottle. Although the artist has not signed their work it is undoubtedly of an excellent standard and will command a good price. £200-250. $285-360

The landscape around Guilin in southern China with its peculiarly shaped mountains is the inspiration behind this lovely bottle painted in a modern style. £180-200. $260-285

The artist of this wild animal bottle has captured the fast moving cheetah and gazelle with incredible accuracy especially taking into account the restrictions within which the painting was carried out. The wolves on the opposite side are equally inspired making this a highly desirable bottle. £400-500. $575-715

An excellent large photographic quality representation of a rhinoceros and a tiger in their natural landscape. Each is beautifully painted. £250-300. $360-430

This superb bottle is by the artist *Ji Hua* (Mrs) and shows in great detail a legendary lady riding a dragon. The story behind this bottle relates to the legend of feeding the dragon with a beautiful virgin each year on the day for celebrating the lives of people who have died. The virgin is seen offering herself willingly during this ceremony. Characters on this face of the bottle read "*ding cou san yue*" which in the lunar calendar equates to March 1997.

On the opposite side the dragon is seen taking away his victim. The date reference is repeated along with the characters "*yu jin men ji hua zuo*" ("painted by *Ji Hua* in Beijing"). *Courtesy of Aisingioro Collection.* £700-800. $1,000-1,145

One of the writers' favorites is this wonderful painting of a vixen with her cubs balanced in the same bottle with an image of two lionesses. Few old or modern bottles are of this quality which would be highly acclaimed in any painted form but is almost unbelievable having been painted under these circumstances. £400-500. $575-715

A superb European style subject inside a beautifull glass crystal bottle. The elegant landscape includes ladies in Victorian dress with parasols. Typically the bottle is unsigned but the subject matter and the execution of it are rarely seen. £250-300. $360-430

This is a lovely bottle with the inside surfaces painted to resemble the panels of a fan, a traditional place for Chinese paintings. On one side a figure in a brown shirt is seen pulling a horse and the poetic calligraphy reads "*liu tang yu jun*" ("the pond with the willow tree is a bath for this beautiful horse"). "*Ding cou chun nian*" from the lunar calendar equates to spring 1997 and "*song bo lin*" is the name of a village in the mountain which was the home town of the artist *Chang Yue*.

On the other side the man is pulling a horse into a river with the legend "*chun jiang yu jun*" ("the spring river is a bath for a beautiful horse"). The characters "*ding cou zhen nian*" indicate that this part of the painting was completed in the New Year of 1997. These two dates give a clear picture of the time period involved in painting a bottle to this level of perfection. This particular subject is based upon a traditional painting reproduced many times in Chinese art. It is also interesting to note the reference here to the artist's place of birth which is common to many painters. *Courtesy of Aisingioro Collection*. £900-1,000. $1,287-1,430

The extraordinary shape of this heavy glass crystal bottle is a traditional representation of a cloud. It also carries two traditional paintings of children and a complex set of calligraphy. On one side two children are "*tong ran tu*" ("face to face in battle") over a chess game. Two signatures appear for the bottle painter "*Huang Shong*", one red on white, as usual, and the other white on red for "*yin*" and "*yang*" style balance. On the other side the caption "*yong e*" means exactly what is painted "singing to the goose". Although this looks like a girl to western eyes, this would have been the hair style of a boy in the pre-1911 period. Further reference to *Huang Shong*, the bottle painter is accompanied by reference to *Huang Zheng*, the original painter. It would appear that the original was painted in 1989 probably for gallery exhibition, and this bottle was painted in 2001 as a tribute. The common surname may indicate a father and son. £250-300. $360-430

Both sides of this superb bottle show a magnificent eagle. The two characters "*xiong fong*" translate literally as "male wind" but refer to the powerful wind as the bird takes off. The five characters with the signature read "*geng shen nian dong zuo*" which is a lunar reference to the year 2000 and the season of winter when the bottle was painted. Like many western painters' signatures the red chop mark is impossible to read accurately, 4.5" (11 cm). £200-250. $285-360

A superb modern bottle in his own style by the well-known painter *Xu Peng Qi* from Beijing. The free flowing hand of this painter's work attracts high prices. Unusually this bottle has a title "*you jin*" ("a quiet secret place") and the year of painting is given as 1994. The characters also refer to the painting having been done in "*yi*" which is an old word referring to the Capital. Further characters describe the picture on one side as "*zhu lan tu*" being "bamboo and daffodil picture". On the opposite side which has splashes of red the words "*he tang*" describe it as a water lily pond and "*xie xia ri*" tells us that it was painted in the summer. £400-500. $575-715

Incredible detail emphasizes the quality of the work of this young but famous artist *Xu Bu*, one of the well-known *Xu* family of artists from Beijing. The characters "*ba jun tu*" tell us what we already know that the bottle is about eight beautiful horses. Further characters tell us that they were from the great Tang dynasty in the year 627 A. D. and were solely for the Emperor's use. The modesty of the artist is highlighted by the fact that his name only appears in small text after reference to the year 2001 in which the bottle was painted. Larger text reading "*xu shi*" simply means "somebody from the *Xu* family" which is typical of these artistic dynasties. £500-700. $715-1,000

A beautifully executed mountain landscape in winter with subtle detail and shading by artist *Hui Ran* (Mrs). *Courtesy of Aisingioro Collection. Photo by Ma Jun.* £700-800. $1,000-1,144

Titled "The many beauties," this lovely bottle shows precisely that, a triple-decker parade of ladies in flowing robes presumably attending an Imperial function. Little wonder then that artist *Liu Hue* is a *Golden Dragon* prize winner. This award rates him as one of the foremost living inside bottle painters in China. As such a single bottle can command a very high price with the greatest demand being in China itself, Taiwan, and Japan. *Courtesy of Aisingioro Collection*. £1,300-1,500. $1,860-2,145

An elegant and colorful inside painted bottle by artist *Dong Quen* using polished rock crystal. Mr *Dong* is now over sixty years old and produces very few new bottles. *Courtesy of Aisingioro Collection. Photo by Ma Jun.* £700-800. *$1,000-1,145*

A set of four inside-painted rock crystal bottles with delicate panels on each side depicting historic street scenes. £300-400 each. $430-575

A thinly hollowed gray agate bottle forms the rare "canvas" for this lovely inside painted bottle. The semi-opaque nature of the agate leaves a misty image of the dogs painted on the inside. *Courtesy of Klemer Collection*. £500-700. $715-1,000

A fine inside painted rock crystal snuff bottle by *Ding Erzhong*, signed *Gen Zi* (corresponding to 1900), 58 mm. (A) £8,400. $12,015

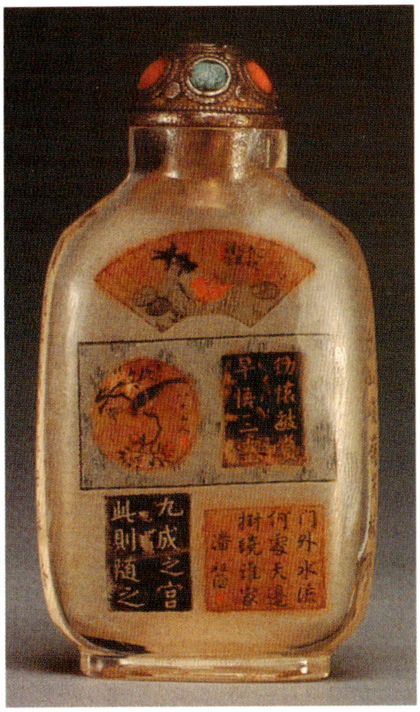

A fine inside painted rock crystal snuff bottle by *Ma Shaoxuan*, twentieth century, 61 mm. (A) £7,650. $10,940

An inside painted rock crystal snuff bottle in the period of Republic Of China (1911-1949), 6.0 cm (2.25"). (A) Estimated at £2,400-4,000. Sold at £13,400. $19,165

A crystal inside painted snuff bottle by *Ye Zhongsan*, 5.7 cm (2.25"). (A) £880. $1,260

A rare and fine inside painted rock crystal snuff bottle by *Ye Zhongsan*, signed *Wu Shen* (corresponding to 1908), 51 mm. (A) £4,800. $6,865

Chapter Nine: Fakes and Forgeries

Here it is important that we state our intention because we have already featured a large number of bottles produced in the twentieth century which some writers and collectors categorize as fakes. In quality, appearance and technique they rank alongside their earlier counterparts and what many lack in age they make up for in affordability.

It has been common practice for centuries in China to replicate the work of earlier craftsmen and even to replicate their marks and signatures but this was not done specifically for gain, in the sense of deceiving buyers, but was considered a sign of great respect to a revered predecessor and referred to as a "nod to the past." In today's market it is unlikely that collectors with a modest budget would be able to own some of the finer snuff bottles of the early Qing period but they can readily afford some of the simpler originals and the later replicas. Reference to the *Victoria & Albert* collection in London and its method of dating bottles shows that, even in a famous collection such as theirs, the only certainty was the date upon which a particular bottle was acquired. What difference then between a good replica made in the nineteenth century and one made in the mid or late twentieth. All buyers would be well advised to exercise caution when buying expensive bottles from whatever source. We have already mentioned that some major auction houses in the West now include twentieth century pieces in their sales with no reference to precise age. Many buyers will assume that the items thus catalogued must have at least some age but this need not be true and once sold they acquire a very valuable provenance. As dealers we have seen this occur on numerous occasions with ceramics, bronzes and furniture.

Clever use of color in this resin bottle makes it look like amber, agate, or cameo glass. It has in fact been carved in the same way as any of them would have been to the shape of a fish swimming among lotus. Is this an attempt at deception or simply the carver's adventure into modern materials? £25-30. $35-40

The very poor quality of this blown glass bottle is not the work of an amateur artist but of the photographic faker. The inability of the bottle to take an accurate image in the process is reassuring for those of us who collect inside painted bottles because we are hardly likely to be lured into buying one of such appalling quality. If you must buy one do not pay more than £5. $7

What concern us more here are materials which replicate the real ones and so may be used to deceive the buyer irrespective of any claims of age. The wide range of resin based materials available today make it possible to replicate almost anything and, indeed, the end products can be an attractive addition for the collector on a modest budget. In China, the unsuspecting tourist may well be sold fake materials, and then rush back to have their bargain assessed, but they will rarely have paid more than a small tourist price for the article. In the West, however, where larger money is at stake, some dealers will undoubtedly try to deceive or, in some instances, not even know the difference themselves.

In the case of inside painted bottles, in particular, many incredulous observers and even some supposed experts suggest that the feat they are observing is impossible and must have been achieved with a transfer. However much it may astound all of us inside painting is both possible and expertly carried out to this day. The suggested application of a transfer would be even more difficult than the painting which astounds us, since the small neck of the bottle would render it impossible to control. As we have already mentioned, in the chapter on inside painting, a small number of tourist bottles have been produced using a photographic technique. The quality of image and the control of color in these bottles is so poor that they should not deceive anyone. They are of such a low standard that, were they painted, they could only have been done by rank amateurs and, as such, would not command anything other than a nominal price.

Anyone even remotely experienced in looking at the work of inside bottle painters will quickly be able to distinguish between the various qualities. From this it is a small step to comparing the prices of the mass-produced ones and those with real merit.

Some of the most common fakes are the creamy colored resins intended to look like ivory. These ivory look-alikes have featured in Western collectibles for around a hundred years, providing the faces and hands for small statuary of the Edwardian and Art Deco periods and many holiday souvenirs from Far Eastern trips. Known commercially as *Ivorine* and *Ivorex,* they have found favor again with restrictions in the movement and sale of the real thing. Some have grain detail in them achieved by stretching the semi-cooled material to create streaks of contrasting color. A more obvious ivory substitute is bone though in this respect we must be careful because bone has always been a material used in its own right for bottles of less importance.

We have already mentioned the likelihood of encountering reconstituted amber, which is now common even for jewelry, and resin amber substitutes as well as copies of cinnabar lacquer. These materials are usually molded and tend to exhibit signs of air bubbles trapped in the process. As they are produced for cheapness there is also usually very little care taken in the finishing, even when they are re-carved, so quality can once again be used as a key identification factor. If in real doubt a small knife or a red-hot needle will usually reveal the truth. While a hot needle will penetrate real amber it will not produce the acrid smell associated with plastics. Done carefully and in a discrete place these tests should not cause any serious damage but may reveal a bargain or prevent a mistake.

It is probably unfair to dismiss plastics or resins totally because they are a modern material which is not always abused for fakery. Some of the bottles illustrated have taken a great deal of skill to produce and deserve some recognition in their own right. Provided they are sold as what they are, and the price is appropriate, they are a valid addition to a modern collection.

One type of faking, which can occur with all materials, is "distressing" or exaggerated wear and tear. Repeated useage over many years creates a unique gentle rubbing and patination. Where the patina has been artificially introduced, the surface looks overdone. Chemicals and excess dirt may be added as well to simulate age-related grime. One such chemical is potassium permanganate, which gives a brown, dirty appearance particularly on ceramics, but when in contact with water turns purple.

The illustrated examples can now tell their own story, but it is clear that many fakes are as attractive to look at and even handle as the ones they are imitating.

This rich looking dark bottle appears when handled to be amber or a highly polished burr wood. The weight precludes it from being any other material which might occur naturally. Close examination of this lovely bottle however, reveals that it is in fact plastic. Its quality denies its material and should be included in a comprehensive collection. £15-20. $21-30

It is difficult to believe that this beautiful bottle can be anything other than what it appears to be. Colored like coral and carved like coral it is, in fact, plastic. Partially molded but finished with hand carving for authenticity it will certainly fool many people. £25-30. $35-40

Chapter Ten: Care and Display

Having embarked upon a collection of snuff bottles it is important to consider their display carefully. As relatively small objects they can be a problem, especially when it comes to security and keeping them clean. The Emperors of China kept most of theirs out of sight in specially made boxes but this is hardly satisfactory today when we like to view our collections and show them off to friends and fellow collectors. Their very existence, apart from storing what is now an unfashionable powder, was designed to delight the senses of both owner and admirer.

Glass display cases with mirror backs and/or sides are particularly suitable and the use of wooden or plastic stands will enhance them by varying the levels. We have attempted to show the benefits of various types of small stand throughout the book and these can readily be found from specialist suppliers and antique shops. Lighting is important and can be added to an existing cabinet or incorporated into the design of one built for the purpose. If lights are used it is important to remember that they produce a dry heat, which may be detrimental to some types of bottle, so a small source of moisture is advisable. A small bowl of water, topped up regularly, should suffice but if any evidence of cracking is observed then additional measures should be taken. At this stage it is probably wise to seek the advice of an established collector or specialist dealer.

A collector friend recently sent a photograph of her pride and joy displayed neatly on glass shelves spanning her bathroom window. Her collection included both overlay glass and inside painted bottles and the light from it may have seemed ideal. Far from it. As they were on an open shelf the repeated need to move the bottles for cleaning greatly increases the risk of damage from chipping but on a more serious note the strong light and heat from the window, added to the dampness of the bathroom, would quickly damage the inside painted bottles. Strong sunlight would cause the color to fade and possibly flake and the dampness could result in mould developing if the stopper seals were not perfect. Even some stone bottles such as turquoise, amethyst and coral will suffer irreparable damage from strong light and heat.

It really doesn't matter whether a collection has cost thousands of pounds or not, it is there to be enjoyed, so display and long term care are important. It is also useful to get the bottles out regularly to examine them and learn about them. Many collectors find it fun to enhance their display, not only with stands but with one or two old tins or containers of snuff and perhaps some snuff saucers or bowls. Old Chinese photographs of people, who may well have been snuffers, make another interesting addition and give visitors, especially, a glimpse into this mysterious world which as a collector you have entered.

Bibliography

Aisin-Gioro, Pu Yi. *From Emperor to Citizen: The Autobiography of Aisin-Gioro Pu Yi*. Beijing: Foreign Languages Press, 1989.

Keverne, Roger (Consultant Editor). *Jade*. London, New York: Anness Publishing Ltd., 1991.

Kleiner, Robert. *Chinese Snuff Bottles*. New York: Oxford University Press, 1994.

Li, He. *Chinese Ceramics: The New Standard Guide*. London: Thames and Hudson Ltd, 1996.

Perry, Lilla, S. *Chinese Snuff Bottles: The Adventures & Studies Of A Collector*. Rutland, Vermont and Tokyo: Charles E. Tuttle Company, Inc., 1960.

Rawson, Jessica (Editor). *The British Museum Book Of Chinese Art*. London: British Museum Press, 1992.

Stevens, Bob, C. *The Collector's Book Of Snuff Bottles*. New York: John Weatherhill, Inc., 1976.

White, Helen. *Snuff Bottles From China: The Victoria And Albert Museum Collection*. London: Bamboo Publishing Ltd., in association with the Victoria and Albert Museum, London, 1992.

Xia Gengqi, Zhang Rong, Chen Simin, and Luo Yang. *Masterpieces Of Snuff Bottles In The Palace Museum*. Beijing: Forbidden City Publishing House, 1995.

Index